IRONPOWER PUBLISHING

HOW TO DRAW
ANIMALS

In Simple Steps For Kids
Tutorial by E.G. Lutz

All Rights Reserved.

With the exception of photocopying and printing for personal use only, no part of this publication may be reproduced in any form or by any means, including scanning, photocopying, or otherwise without prior written permission of the copyright holder.

Copyright © 2016 IRONPOWER PUBLISHING

PUBLISHER'S NOTE:

Learning to draw animals can be both fun and easy when you are shown correctly right from the start. So why not learn from the master teacher who is credited to have inspired Walt Disney to start drawing and pursue his animating career. Author and illustrator Edwin George Lutz is the man, and he is famous for his method of breaking down complex illustrations into simple step-by-step stages that anyone can follow. Many fine artists and illustrators over the decades have used his technique, and the classic teachings in this book will show you how as well. In this remarkable 152 page course you will learn how to draw a fantastic range of cartoon-like animals. It is divided into 3 sections:- Creatures Of The Land, Creatures Of The Air, and Creatures Of The Water.

Animals included are dogs, cats, horses, elephants, birds, fishes, butterflies, rabbits, monkeys, bears, owls, bees, star fish, pigs, frogs, prairie-dogs, mice, chickens, a camel, cow, crab, dragonfly, fox, giraffe, kangaroo, chipmunk, goat, buffalo, raccoon, sea horse, snail, and a tortoise.

This book is aimed at teaching children (although it's great for any beginner no matter the age), and the choice of pictures is designed to keep a child fascinated. There are over one hundred animals to draw, and the method makes for a magical experience making drawing easy and delightfully interesting.

The book provides a step-by-step system that fixes the object in memory and develops naturally a physical skill and a memorized knowledge of proportion and form. Images are broken down into simple key-lines, which are then built upon with clear step-by-step instructions, resulting in impressive drawings.

Instructions are very brief, for the key-lines of each object tell their own story and the child is entranced by the results soon gained. The youngest child may grasp the magic progress of this way of working and he or she will quickly learn to draw the picture naturally and well.

We think anyone who applies the knowledge contained within this course will be delighted with their results, and the speed and ease at which they attain them.

- Ideal gift for children.
- Learn from this timeless classic that has inspired so many children and adults alike to create their own beautiful works of art.
- Simple to follow, yet for budding artists of all ages leads to enviable drawing skills.
- Step-by-step technique takes a blank page to a finished drawing using principles seen in sophisticated artwork and animations today.
- Fast progression in skill level with this method that uses gradual, simplified stages to build a finished piece of artwork.

TABLE OF CONTENTS

Adjutant.....................118	Flying Fish.....................135
Bears.....................33	Fox's Head.....................50
Bees.....................57	Frog (Tadpoles).....................138
Bob White.....................86	Frogs.....................136
Buffalo.....................49	Geese.....................77
Butterflies.....................61	Giraffe.....................52
Camel.....................53	Goat.....................32
Cat's Face.....................5	Goosling.....................79
Cats.....................2	Herons.....................105
Chicken (Hen).....................69	Horse's Head.....................27
Chicken (Rooster).....................66	Horse (Movements).....................29
Chicks.....................67	Horse (Standing).....................28
Chipmunk.....................22	Humming Birds.....................116
Cow.....................31	Kangaroo.....................51
Crab.....................141	Magpie.....................117
Crane.....................109	Mice.....................42
Crane's Head.....................110	Monkeys.....................40
Crested Crane.....................112	Owl's Head.....................84
Curious Fishes.....................133	Owls.....................80
Dog (Bulldog).....................15	Parakeets.....................87
Dog (Running).....................7	Parrots.....................90
Dog's Face.....................8	Pelican.....................120
Dogs.....................6	Penguin.....................103
Dragonfly.....................60	Pigs.....................24
Ducks.....................70	Prairie-Dogs.....................48
Elephant (Baby).....................37	Rabbits.....................10
Elephant (African).....................36	Raccoon.....................23
Elephant (Asiatic).....................35	Sea Horse.....................142
Elephant (Circus).....................39	Seagull.....................108
Fantail Pigeon.....................115	Snail.....................55
Fish (Angel Fish).....................133	Squirrels.....................19
Fish (Bluefish).....................132	Star Fish.....................143
Fish (Cow Fish).....................133	Stilt.....................119
Fish (Largemouth Bass).....................127	Stork.....................104
Fish (Milkfish).....................130	Swallows.....................92
Fish (Moon Fish).....................133	Swan.....................113
Fish (Red Gurnard).....................129	Thrushes.....................101
Fish (Red Seabream).....................128	Tortoise.....................54
Fish (Shorefish).....................131	Turkey.....................114
Fish (Trunk Fish).....................133	Various Birds.....................121
Flicker.....................107	

ITEMS REQUIRED FOR DRAWING

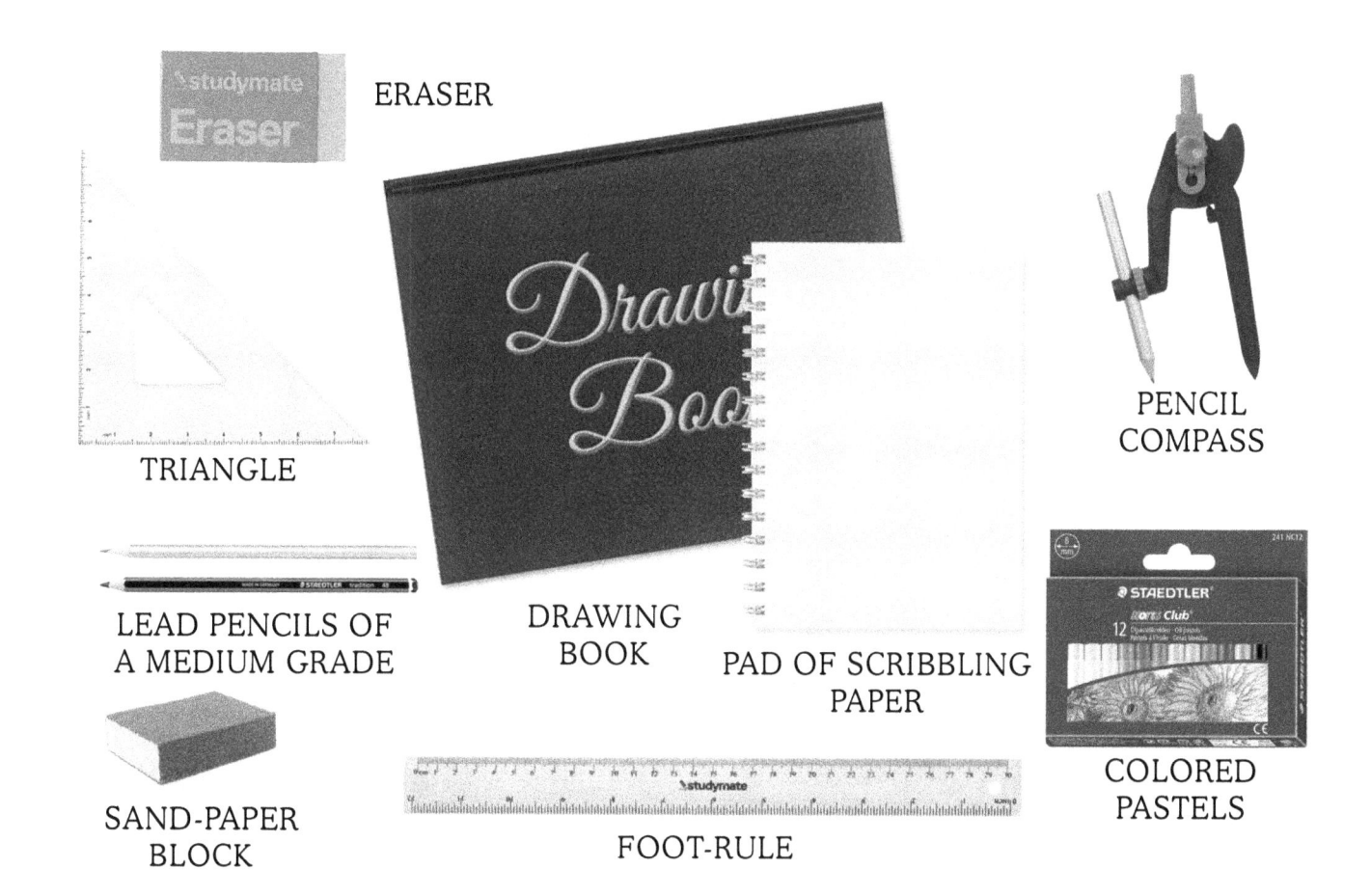

- ERASER
- TRIANGLE
- LEAD PENCILS OF A MEDIUM GRADE
- DRAWING BOOK
- PAD OF SCRIBBLING PAPER
- PENCIL COMPASS
- COLORED PASTELS
- SAND-PAPER BLOCK
- FOOT-RULE

A lead-pencil and a pad of scribbling paper is about all you need in copying most of the pictures in this book. A rubber for erasing would be good to have, too. You might also get a small wooden or plastic triangle, a foot rule, and a compass with a pencil-point.

Point the lead of your pencil on a block of sandpaper, or a pencil sharpener. No doubt you will want a water-color box. It is a good thing to have, but you can get lots of enjoyment in coloring your drawings with pencils, pastels, or crayons.

INSTRUCTIONS

In drawing from this book, copy the last diagram, or finished picture, of the particular series before you.

The other diagram-beginning with number one, then number two, and so on-show how to go on with your drawing. They give the order in which to make the various strokes of the pencil that together form the completed picture. The dotted lines indicate where light lines are drawn that help in construction-that is; getting proportions correctly, outlining the general form, or marking details in their proper places. Do not press hard on the pencil in making these construction lines, then they can be erased afterwards. It is not intended that the dotted lines in the diagrams are to be copied by you as dotted lines. Dotted lines in the diagrams throughout the book merely represent construction lines that are to be marked faintly.

Use a pencil compass for the circles, or mark them off with buttons or disks.

SECTION ONE
Creatures of The Land

CATS

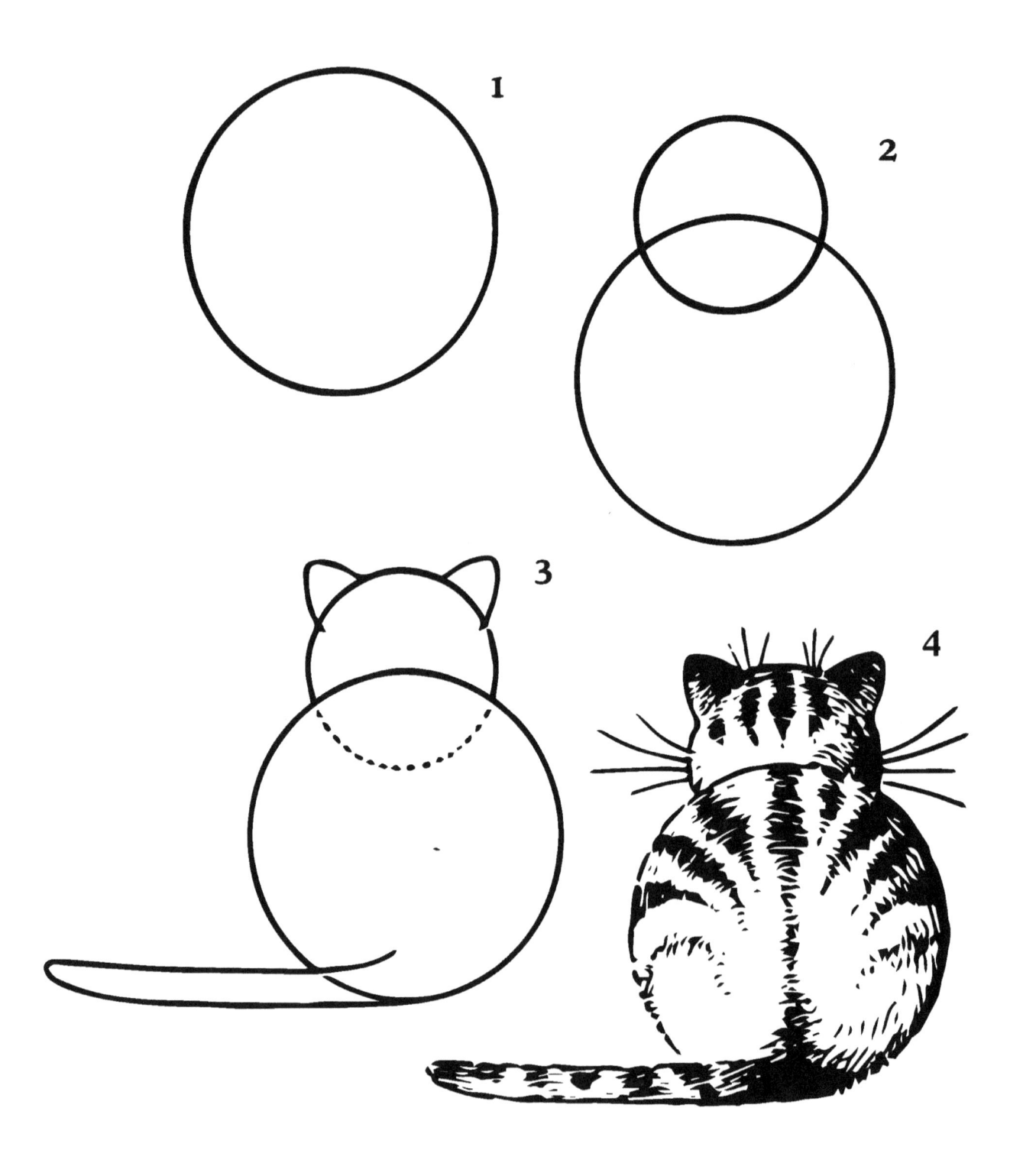

1
2
3
4

1 2 3

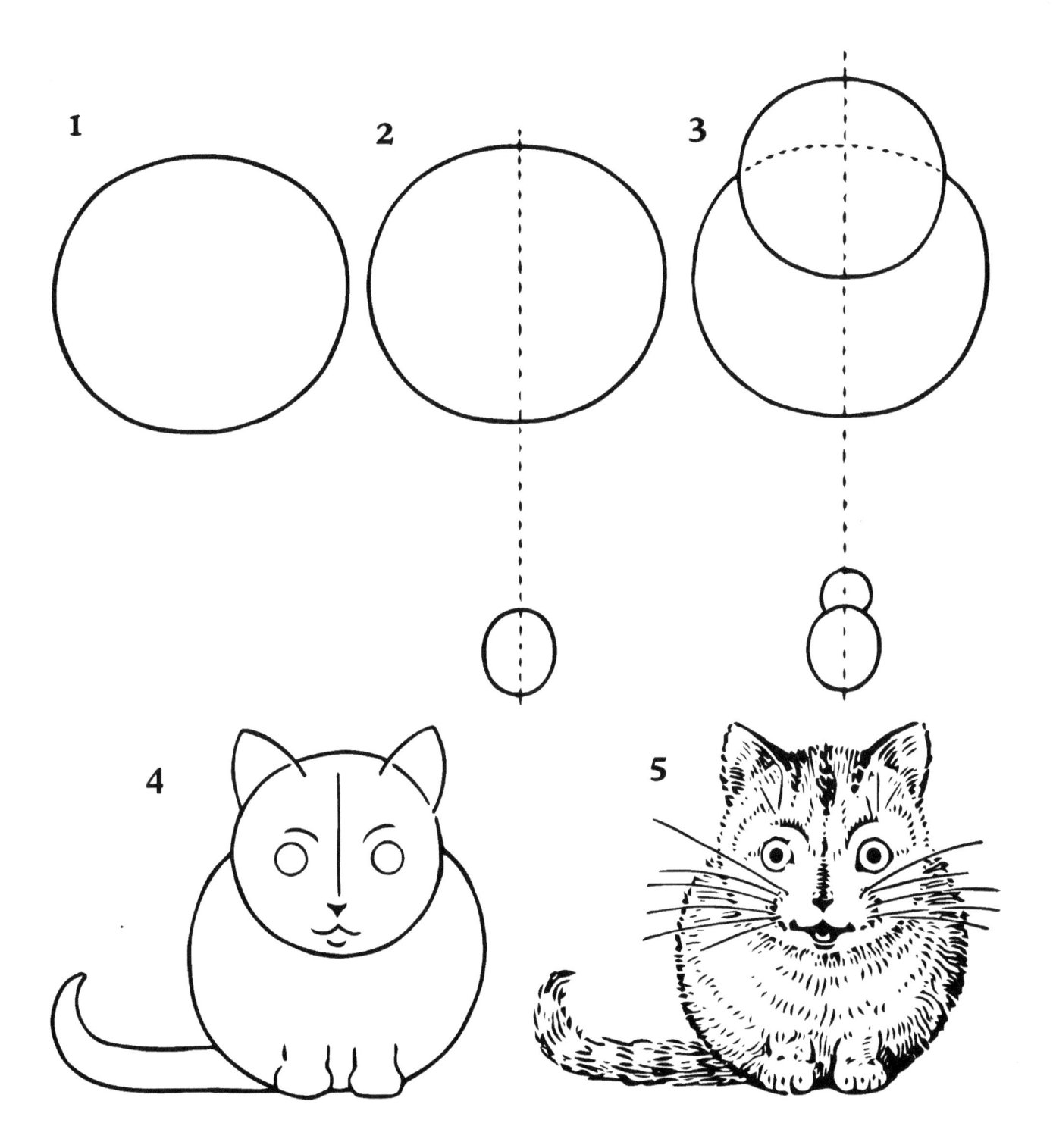

4 5

1

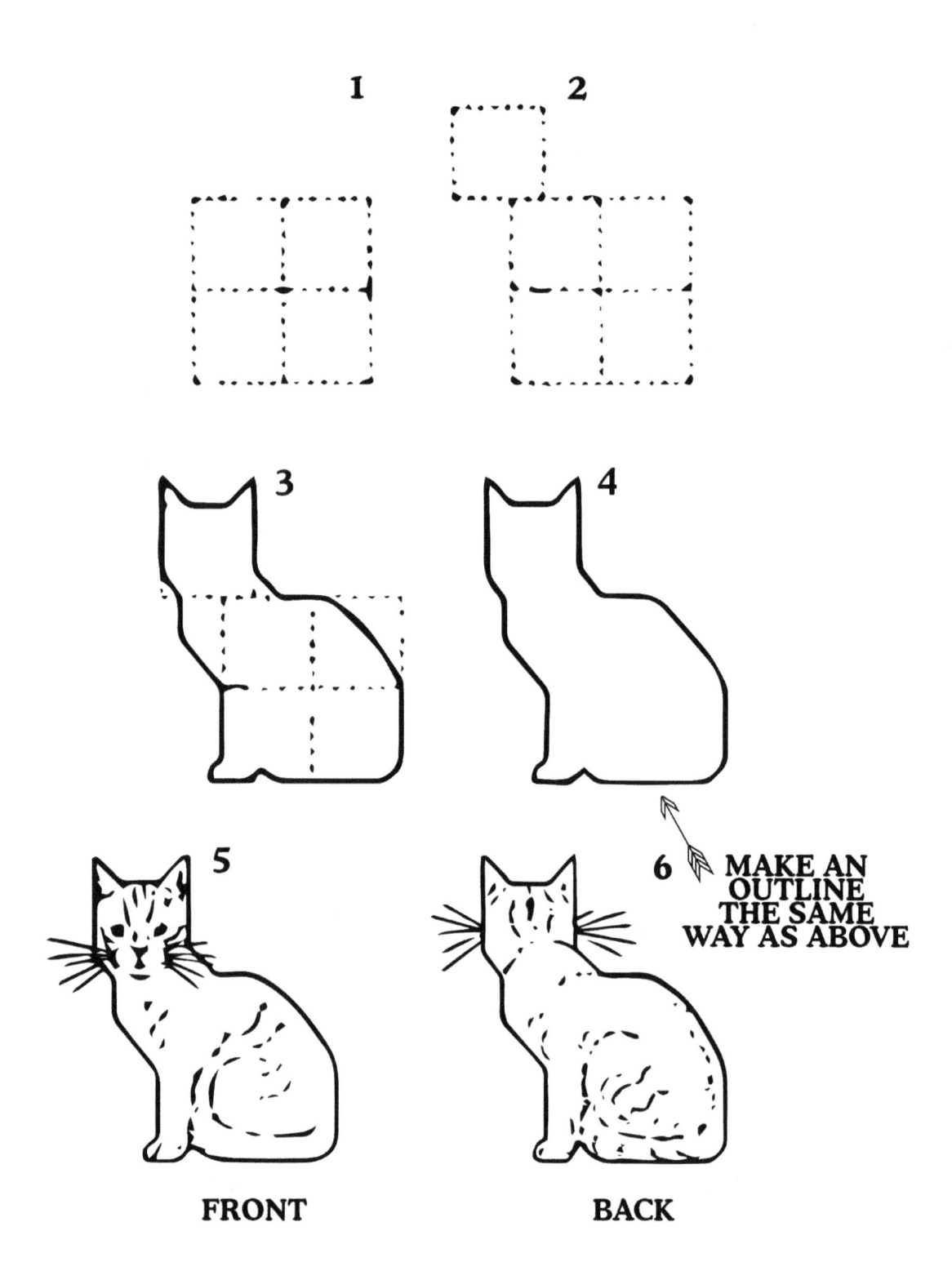

2

3

4

5

6 **MAKE AN OUTLINE THE SAME WAY AS ABOVE**

FRONT

BACK

CAT'S FACE

DETAILS TO PAY ATTENTION TO WHEN DRAWING A CAT'S FACE

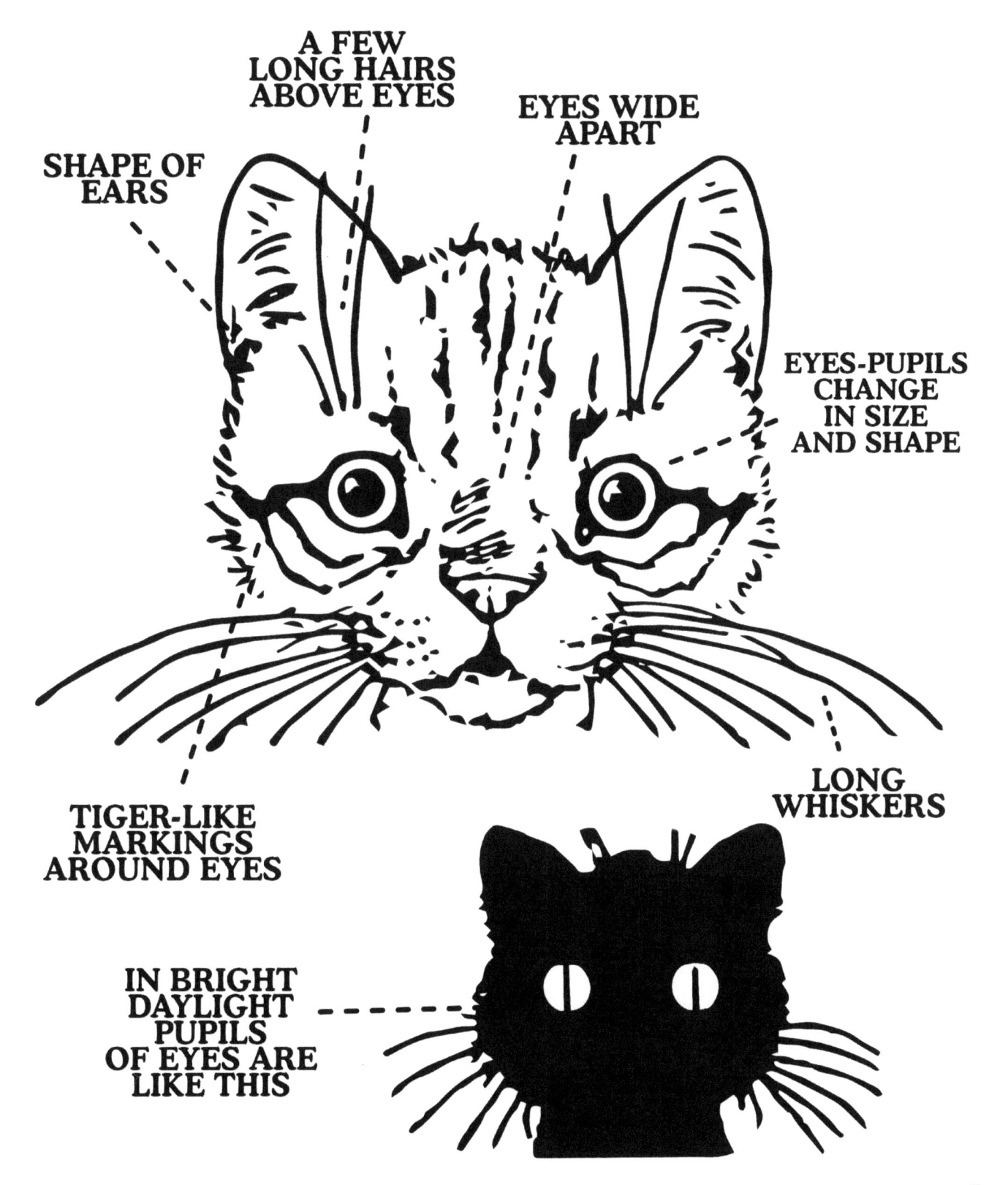

- A FEW LONG HAIRS ABOVE EYES
- EYES WIDE APART
- SHAPE OF EARS
- EYES-PUPILS CHANGE IN SIZE AND SHAPE
- TIGER-LIKE MARKINGS AROUND EYES
- LONG WHISKERS
- IN BRIGHT DAYLIGHT PUPILS OF EYES ARE LIKE THIS

DOGS

RUNNING DOG

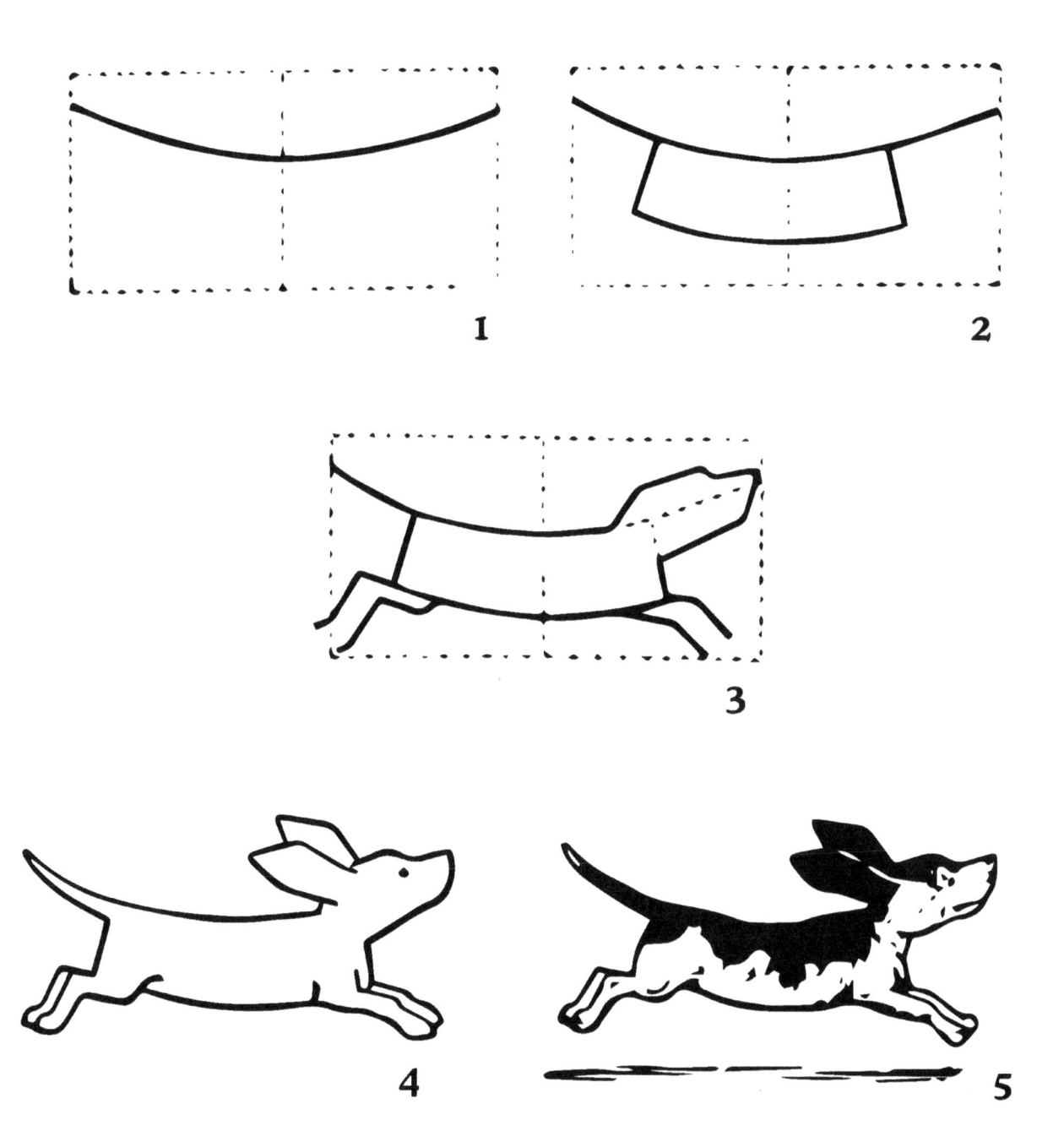

1

2

3

4

5

DOG'S FACE

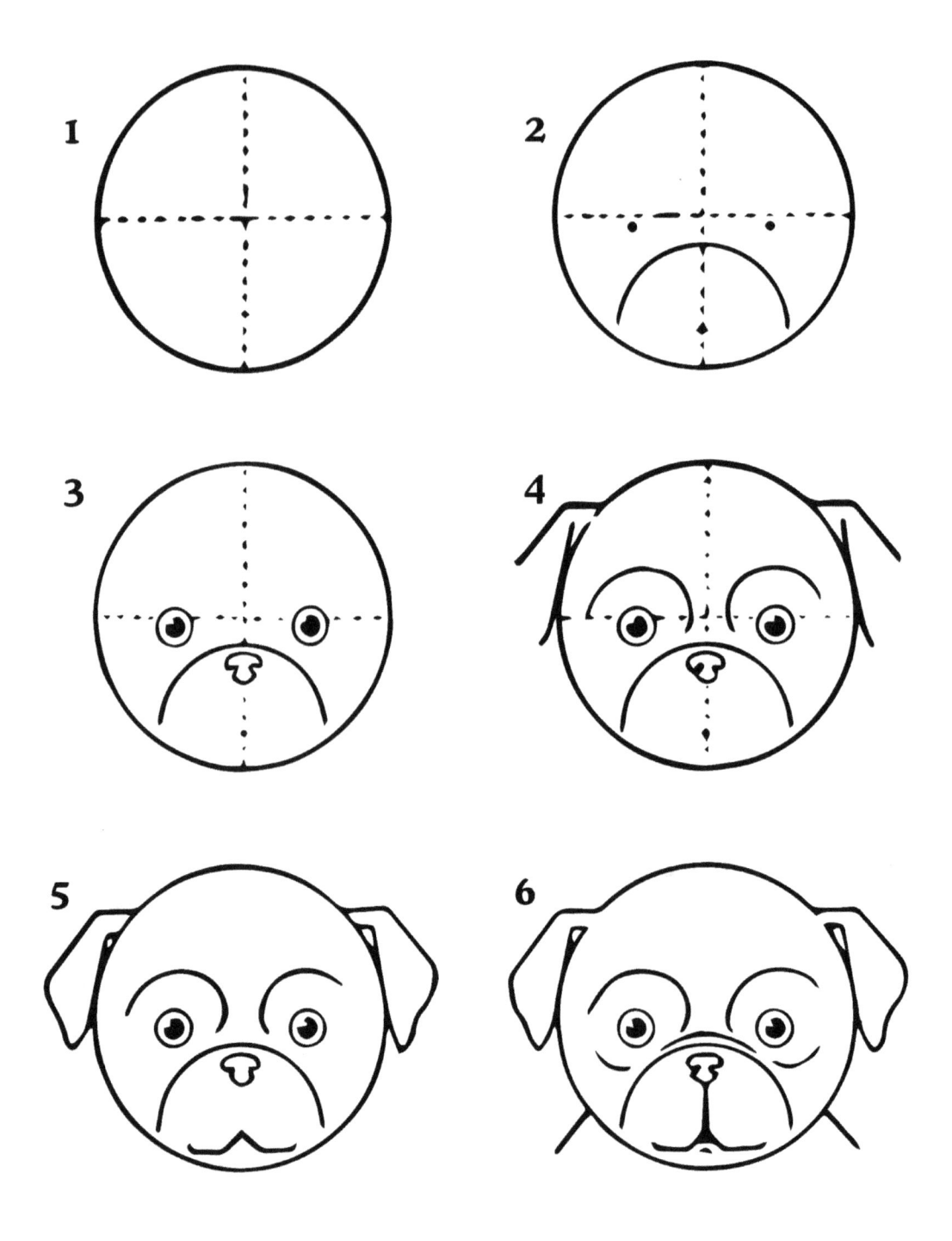

1
2
3
4
5
6

BULLDOG

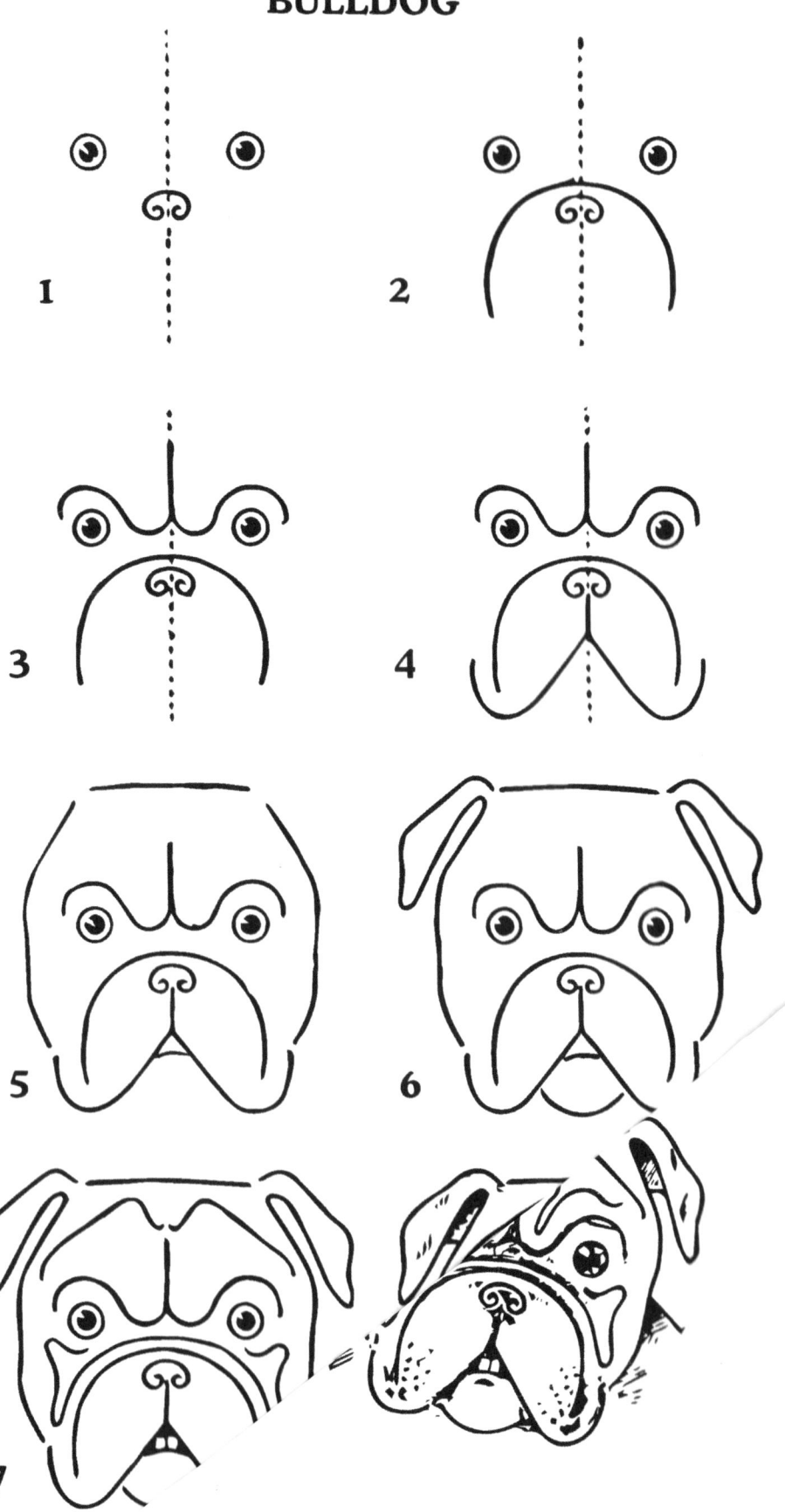

1
2
3
4
5
6
7

RABBITS

1
2
3
4
5

1 2 3

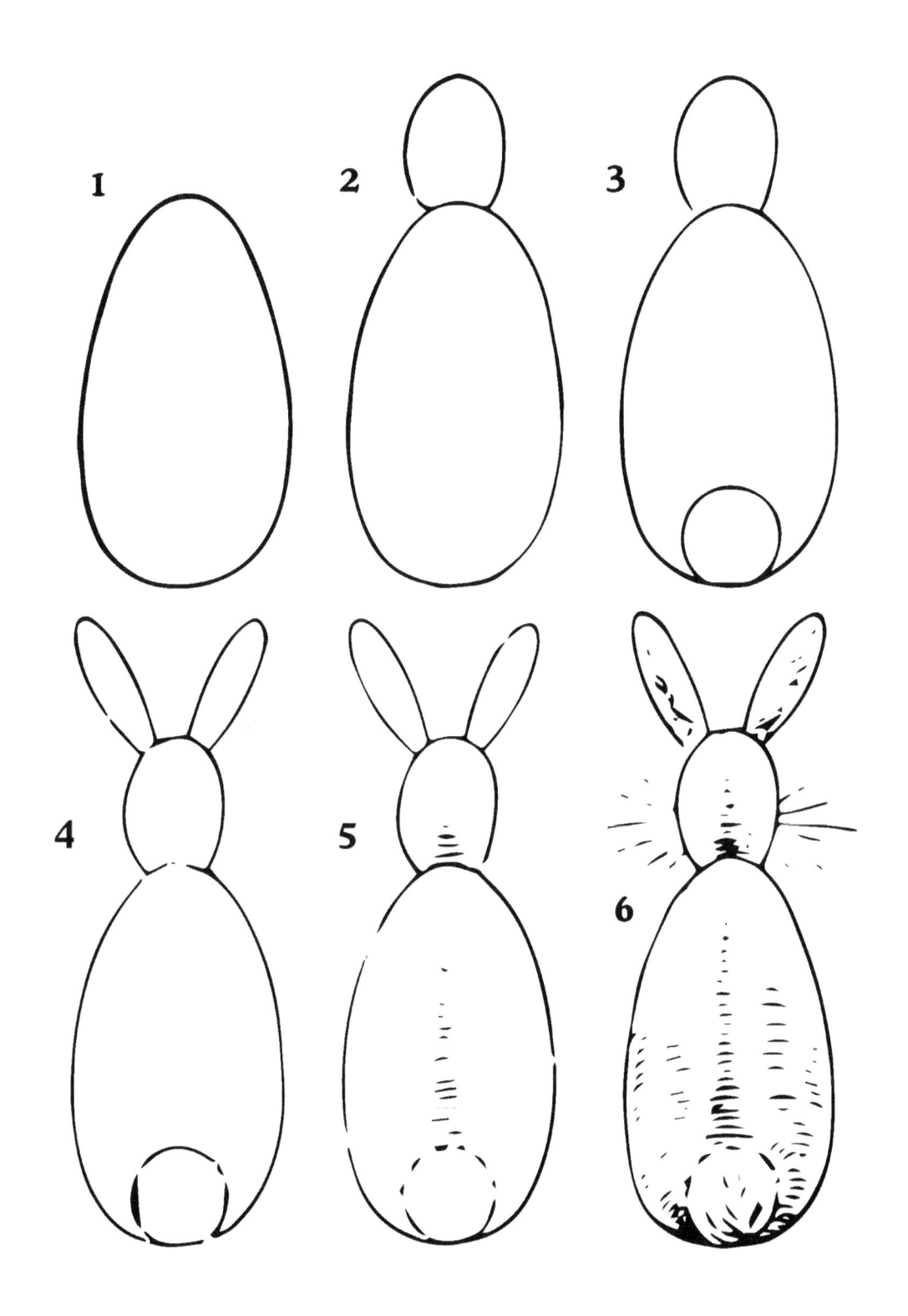

4 5 6

11

1

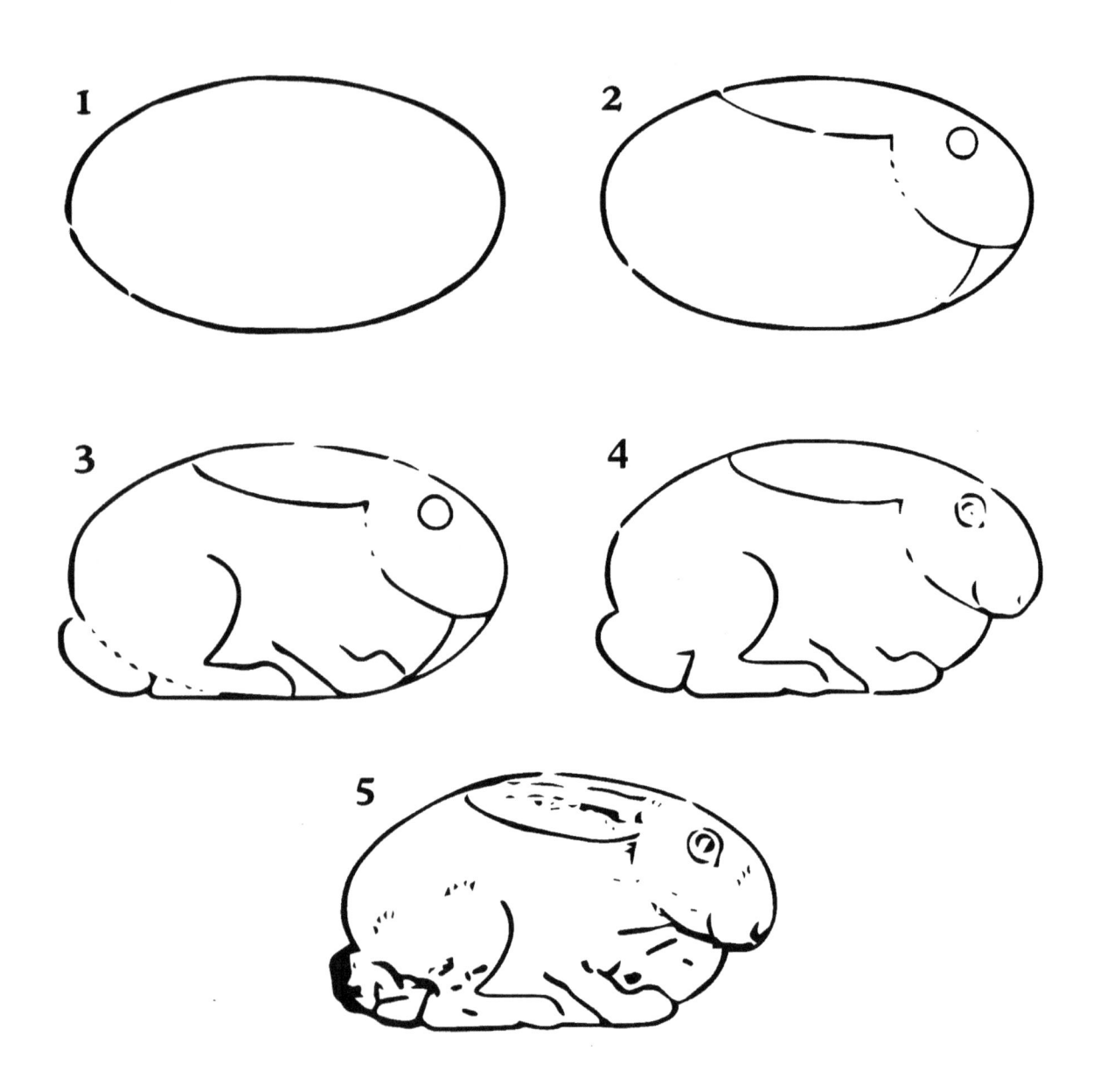

2

3

4

5

1

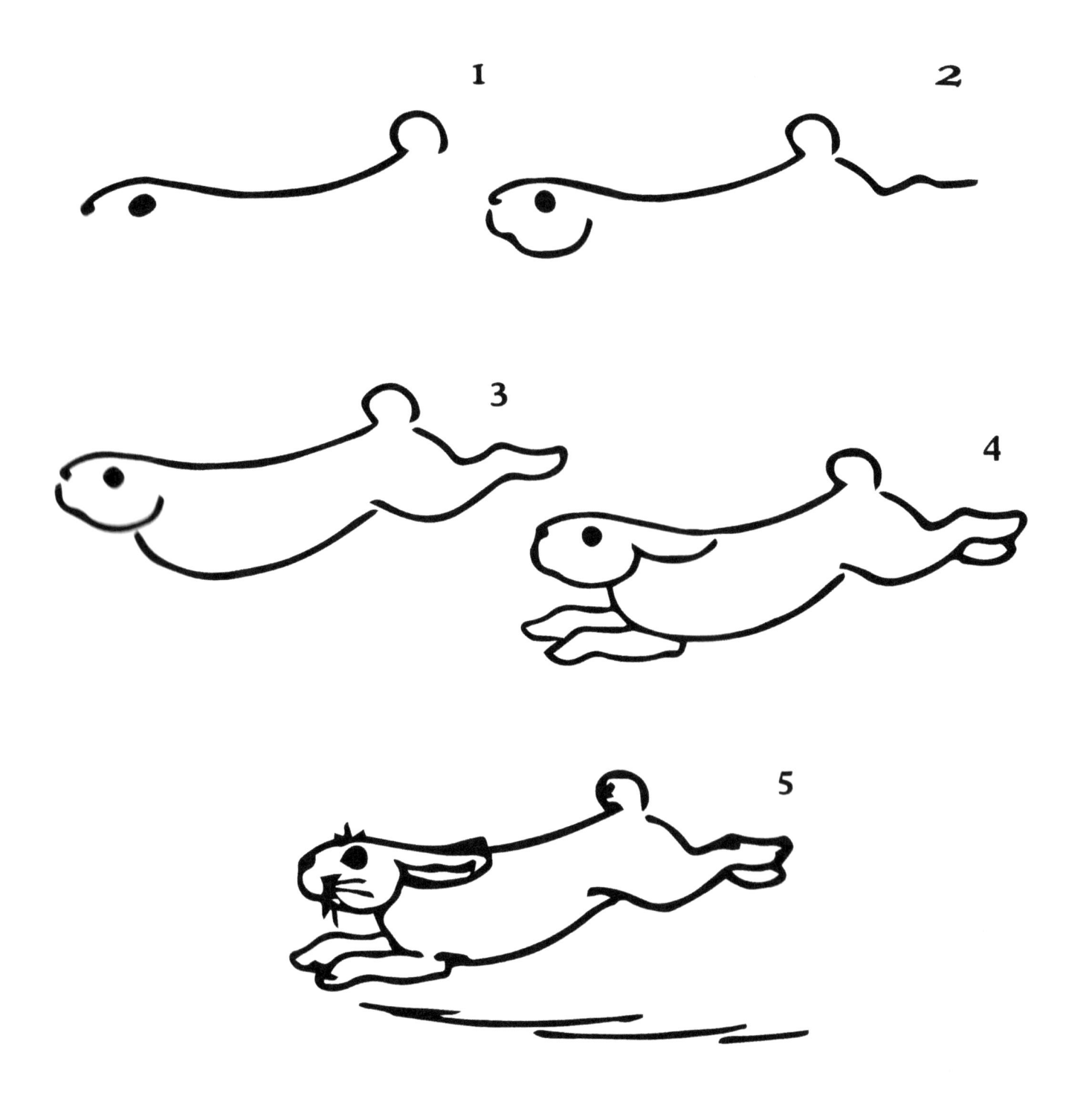

2

3

4

5

1 2 3
4 5 6

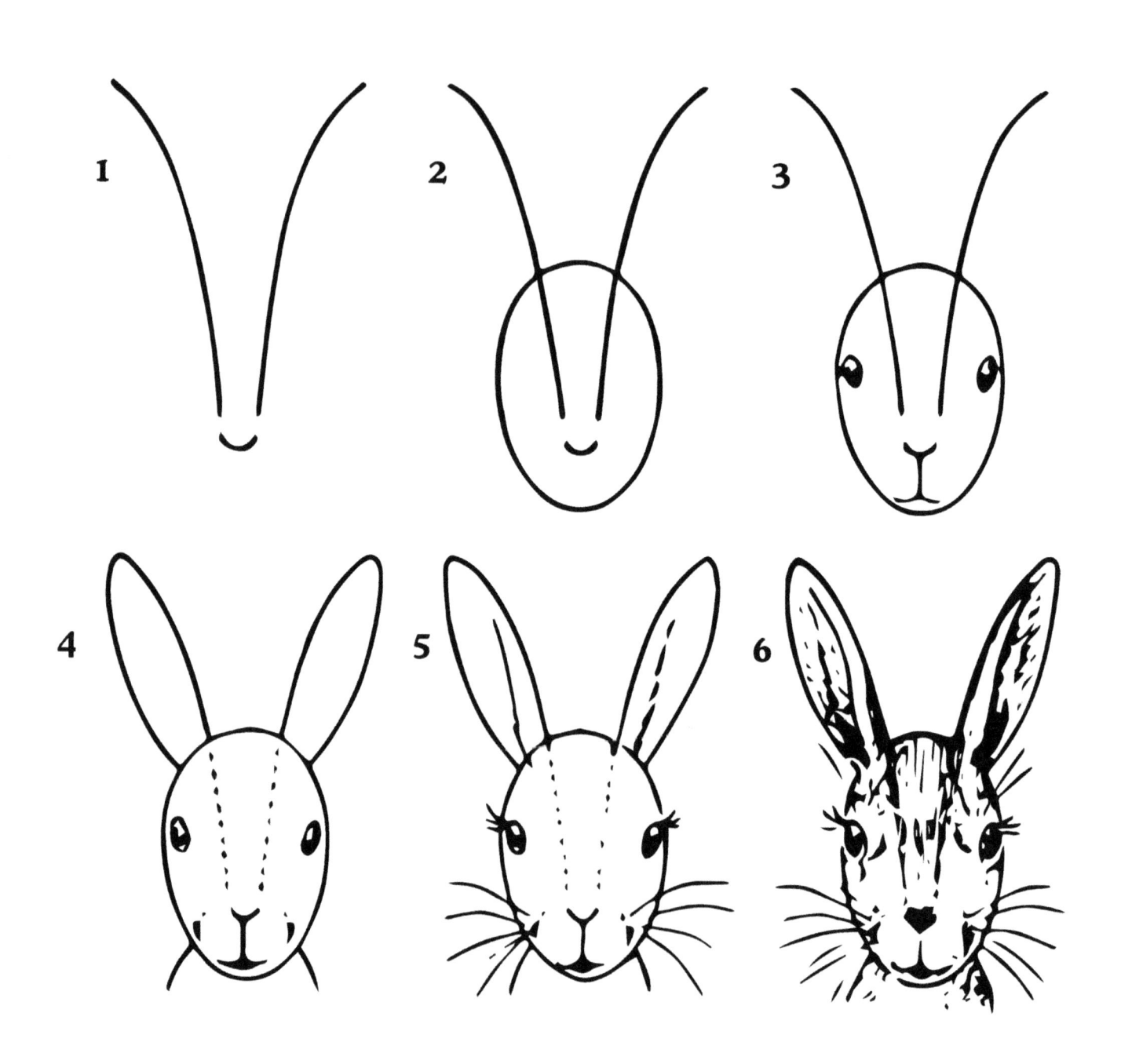

SQUIRRELS

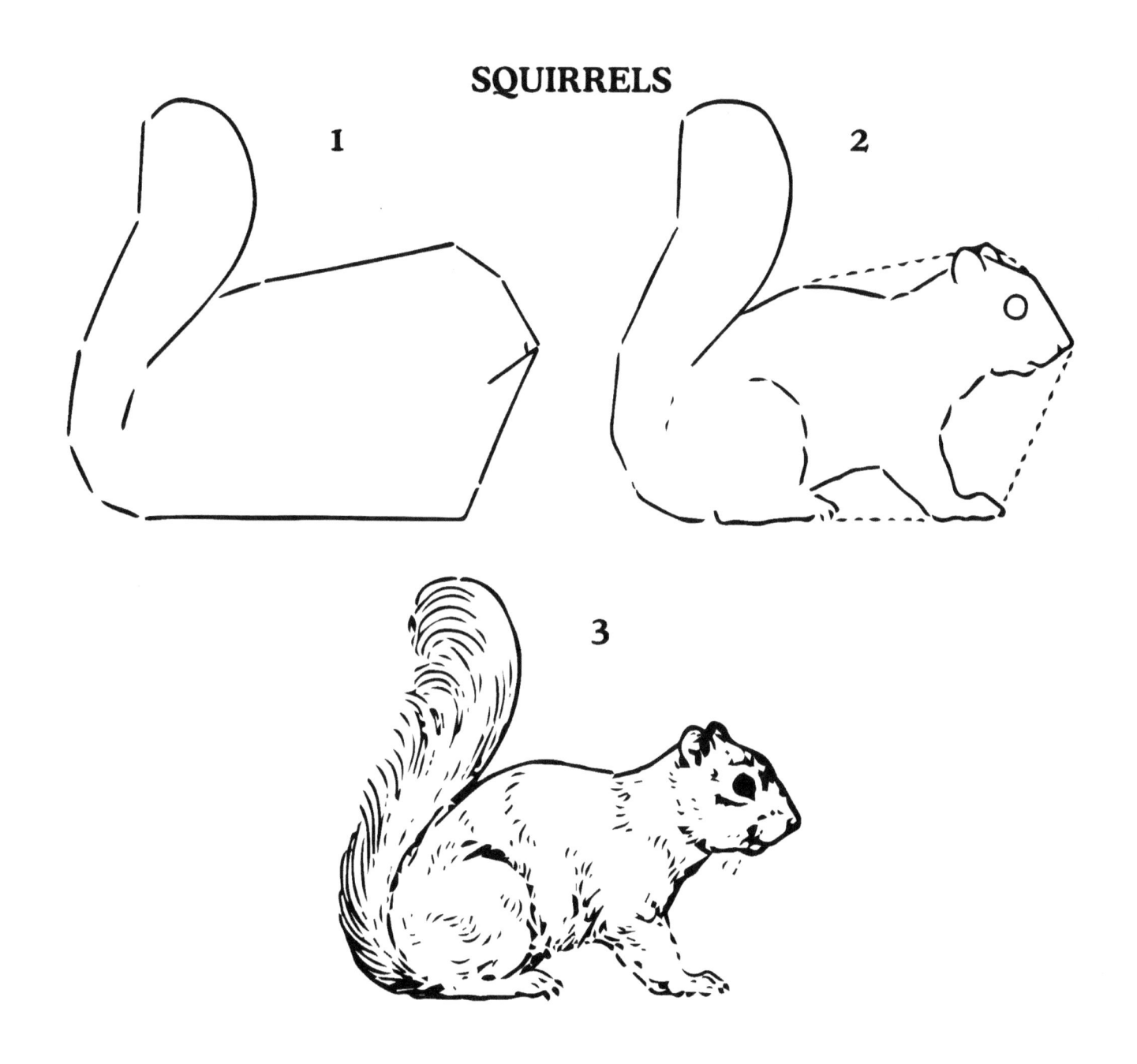

1

2

3

1 2 3

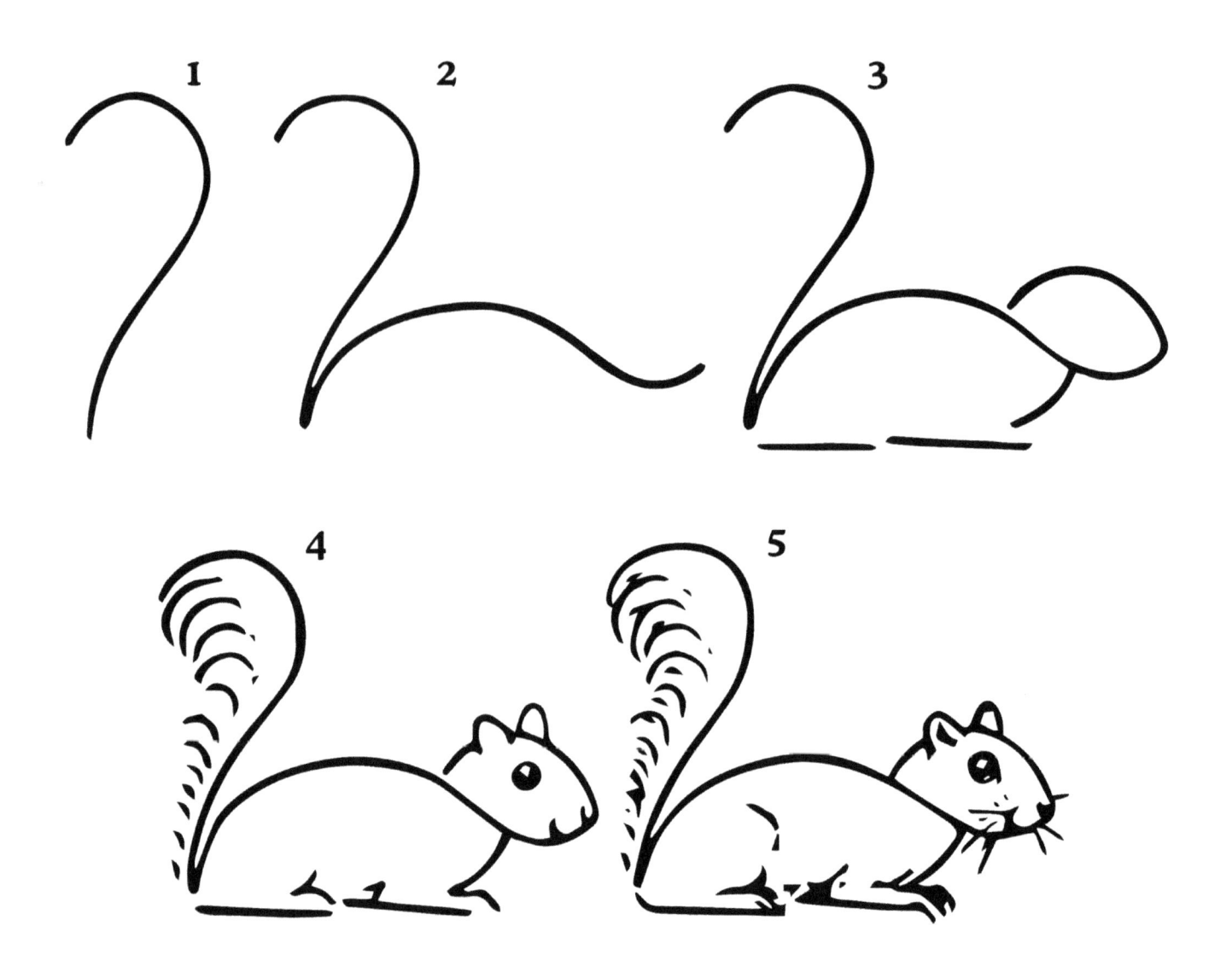

4 5

1
2
3
4
5
6

21

RACCOON

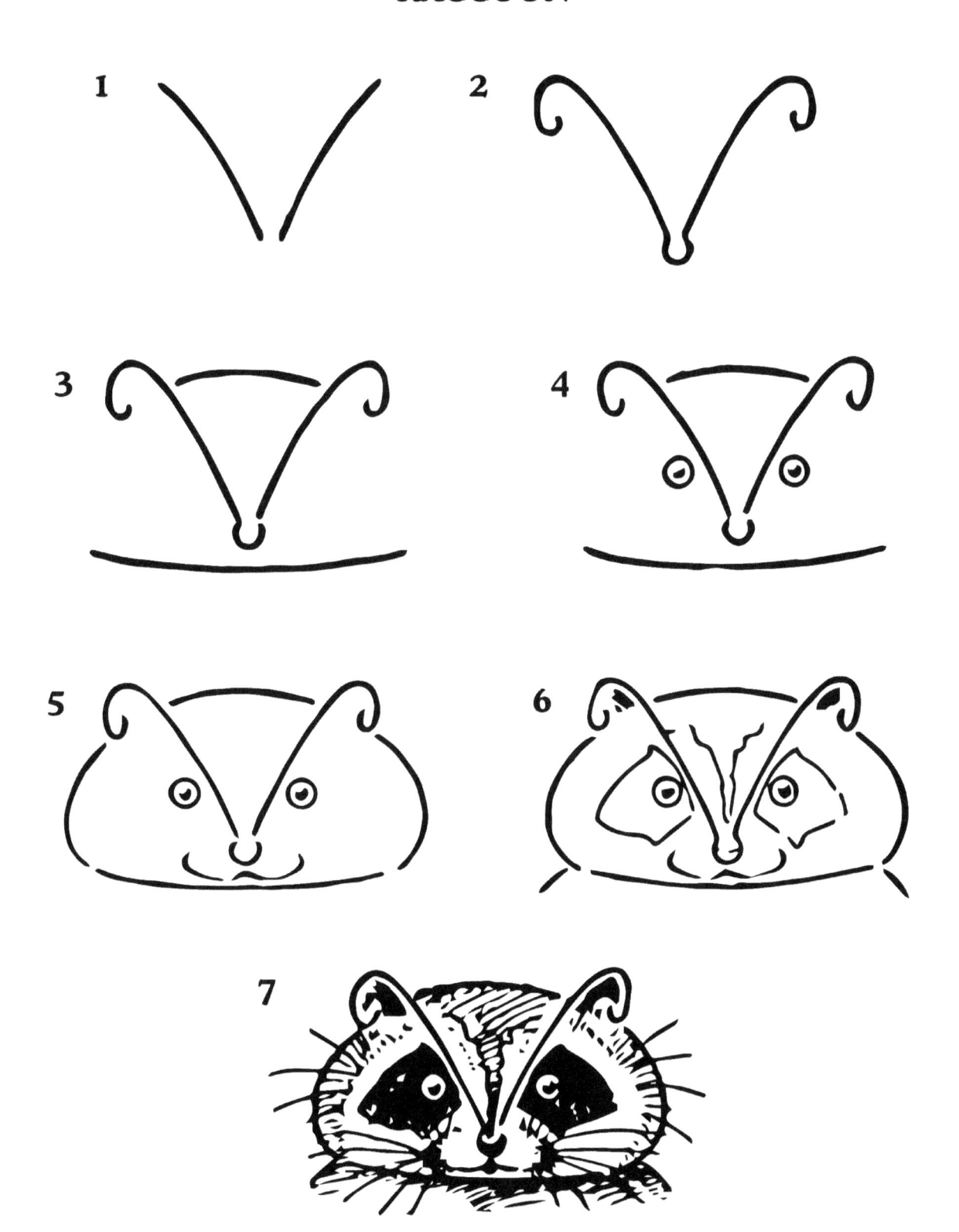

1
2
3
4
5
6
7

PIGS

DRAWING A PIG WITH A SINGLE LINE AND WITH THE EYES CLOSED

Here we have the picture of a pig in a simple outline. It is a copy for you to follow. But you are to make your drawing in a peculiar manner; that is, with the eyes closed, or not looking at the paper, and in one unbroken line. Now, drawing in this way, by which the inner vision only is used, the attention is called to one great fact about drawing. It is this:

Drawing is first a matter of the mind and then only secondly a thing of pencil and paper.

When you are trying this little exercise of drawing a pig with the eyes closed and without lifting the pencil from the paper, so as to get one continuous line you are forced to hold and keep in your mind the picture of a pig. You can understand then that although we need pencil, brushes, and paints in picture making, the first thing needed is an idea or an image in the mind of that which we wish to portray.

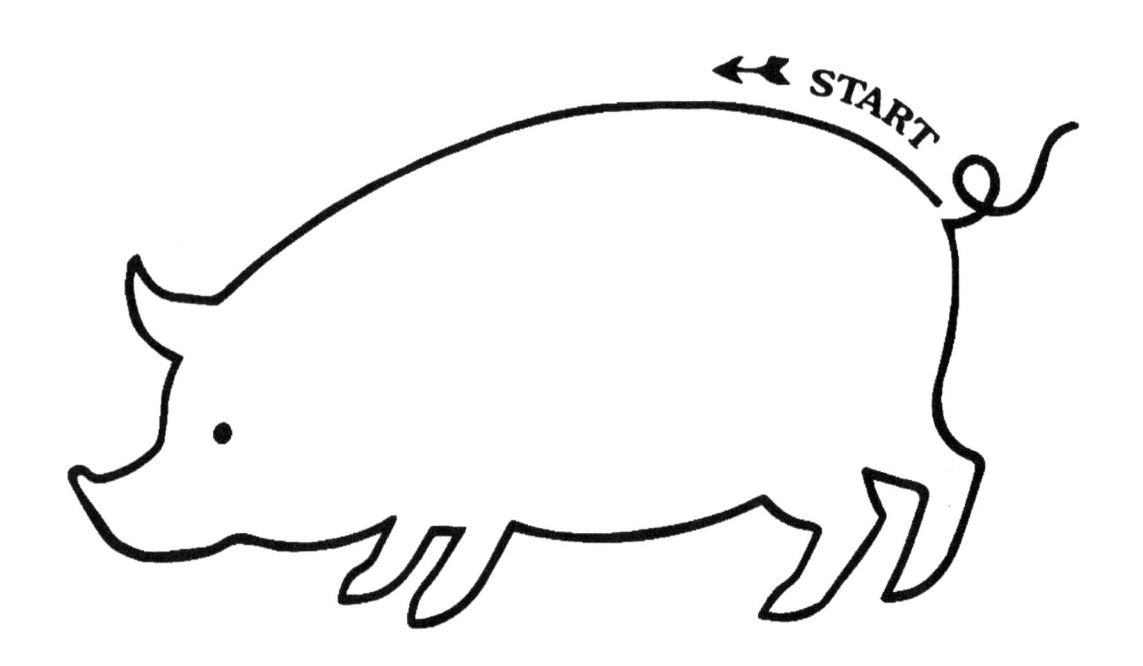

25

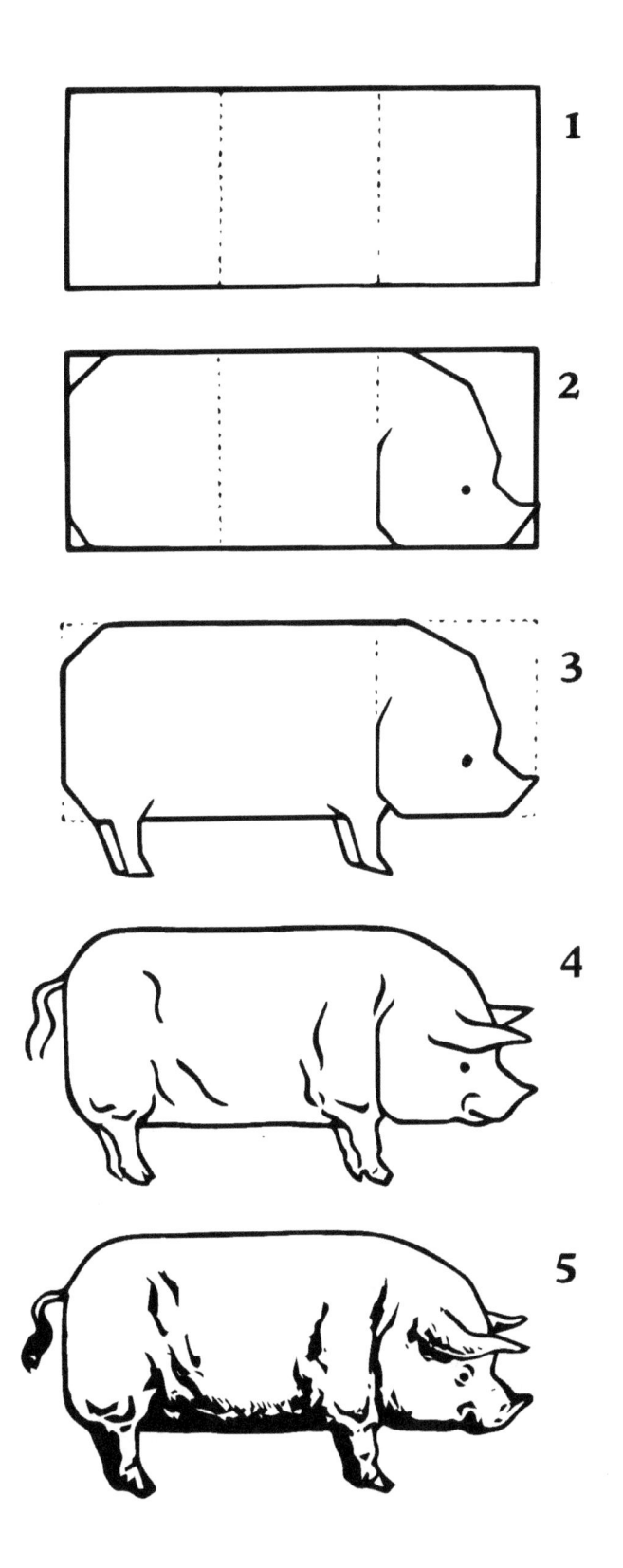

1
2
3
4
5

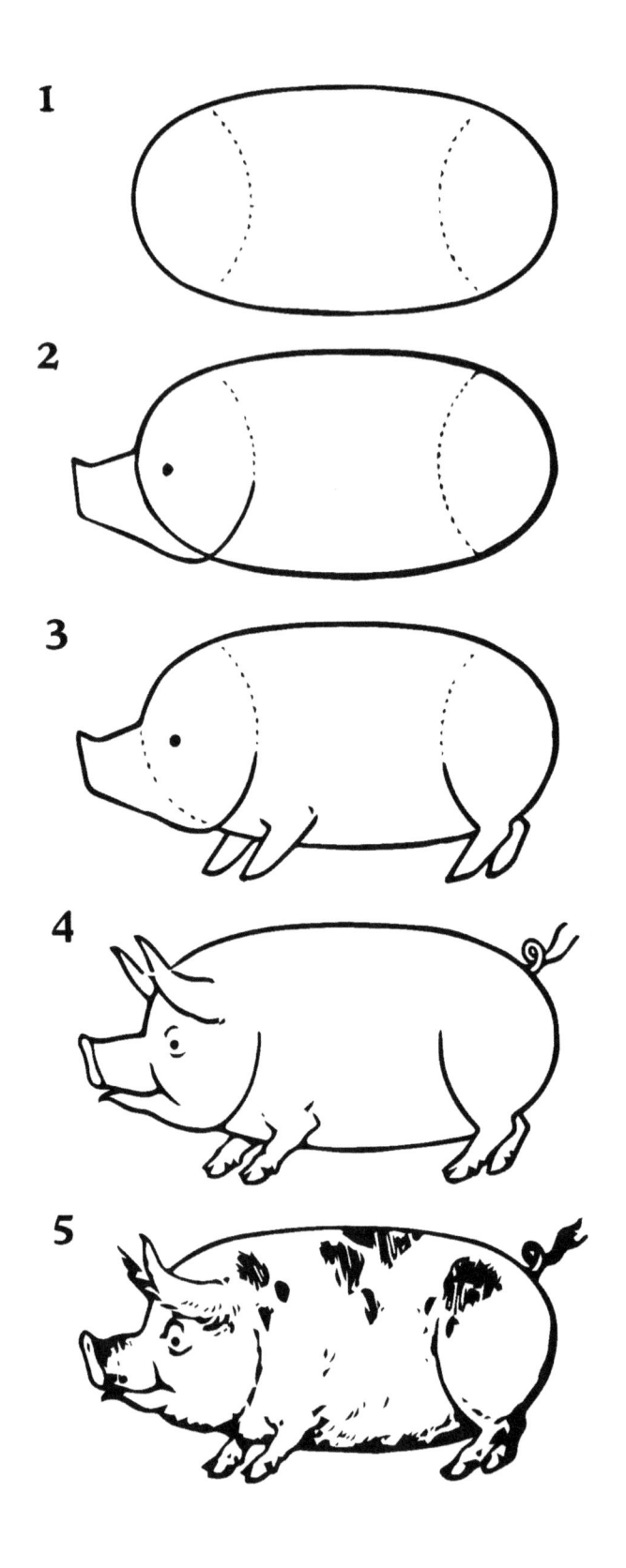

HORSE'S HEAD

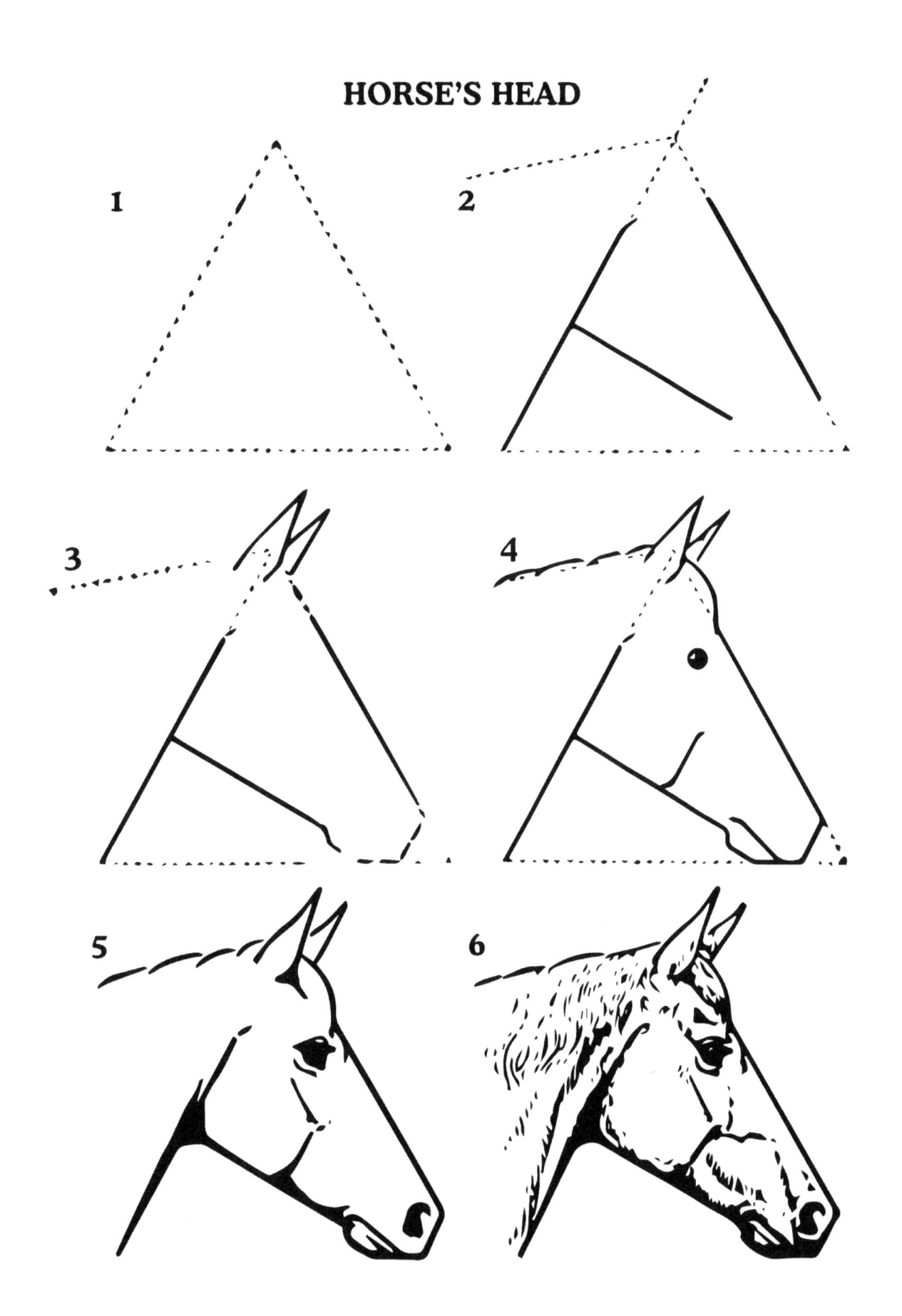

STANDING HORSE

Start your sketch with a square. Draw it free-hand; that is, without the aid of ruler or triangle. Make it as accurately as possible and then divide it into two parts by a line across it just above the middle. Now, in one corner mark a triangle pointing obliquely upward and another triangle slanting downward. The exact procedure is shown above. All the lines that you have been marking so far should be made faintly, as they are only construction lines.

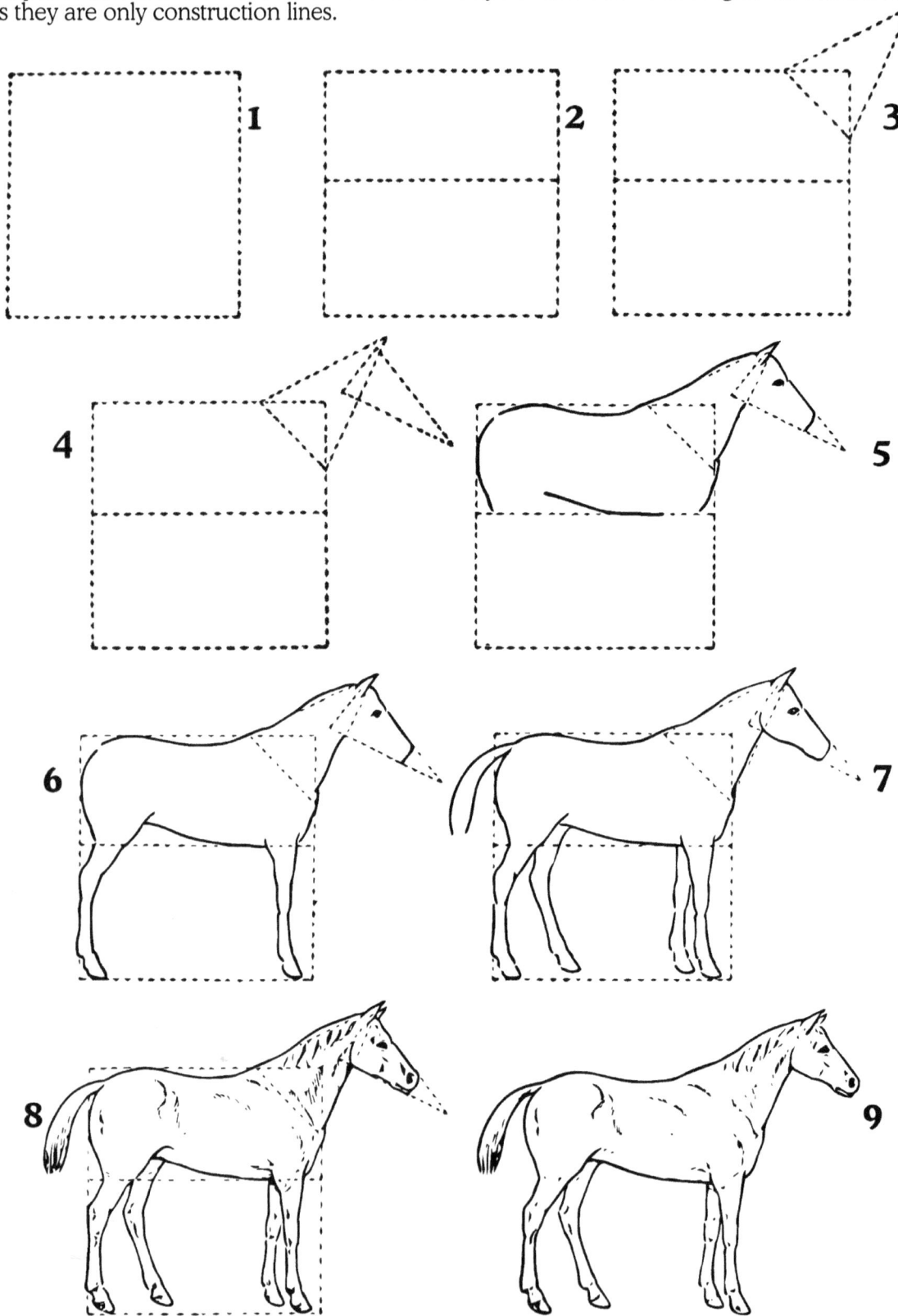

COW

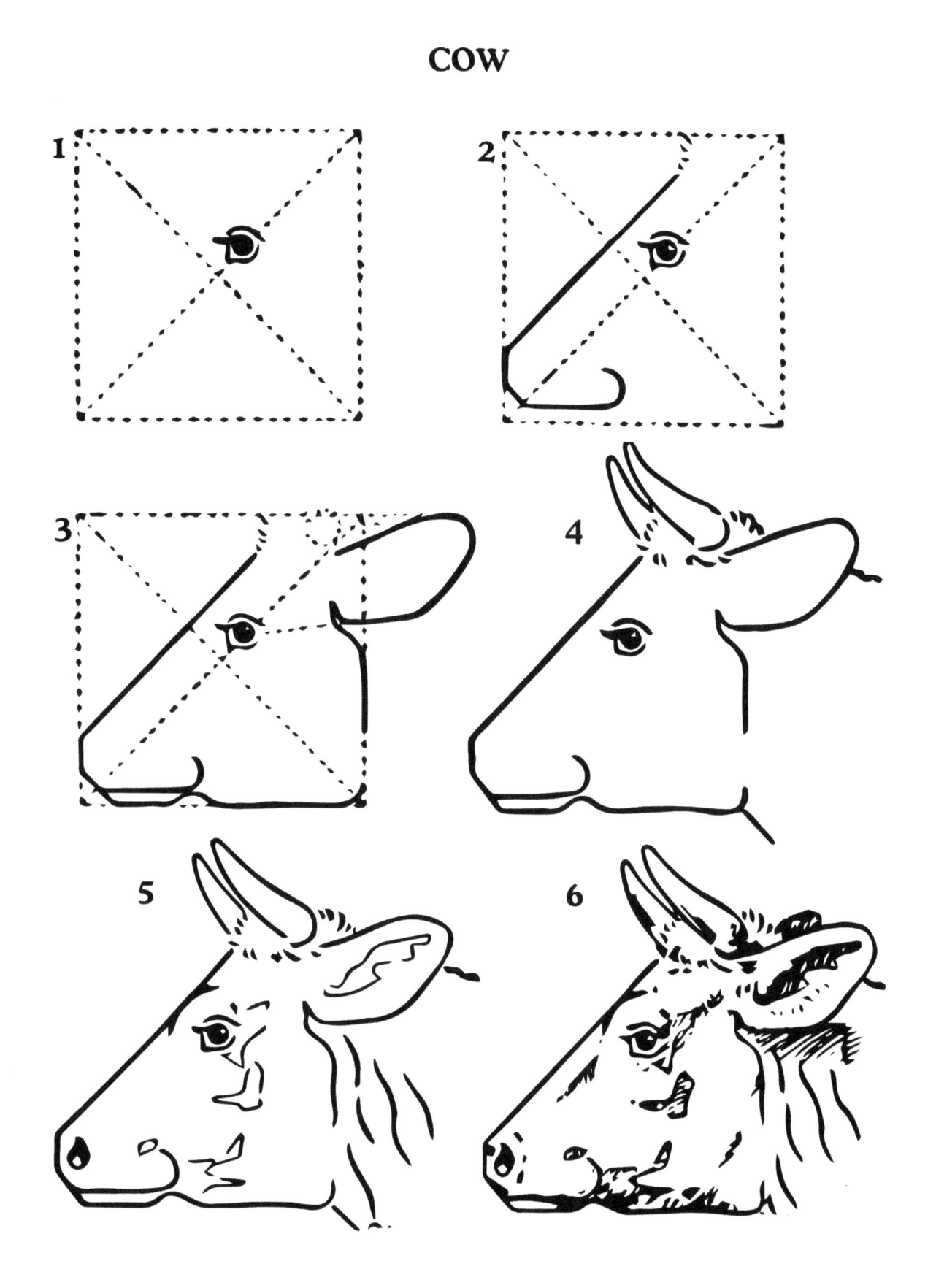

GOAT

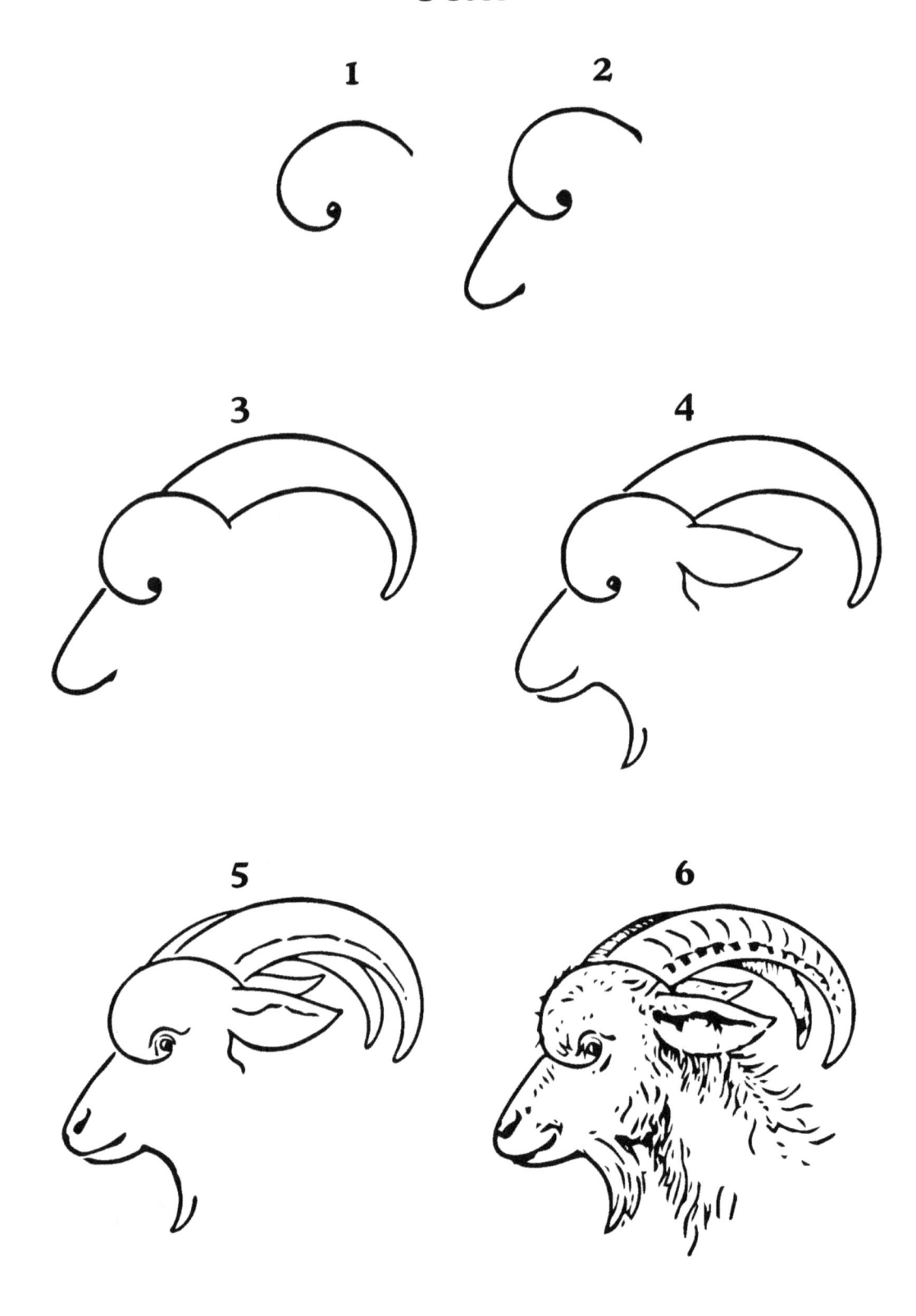

1 2

3 4

5 6

32

BEARS

1
2
3
4
5

1 2

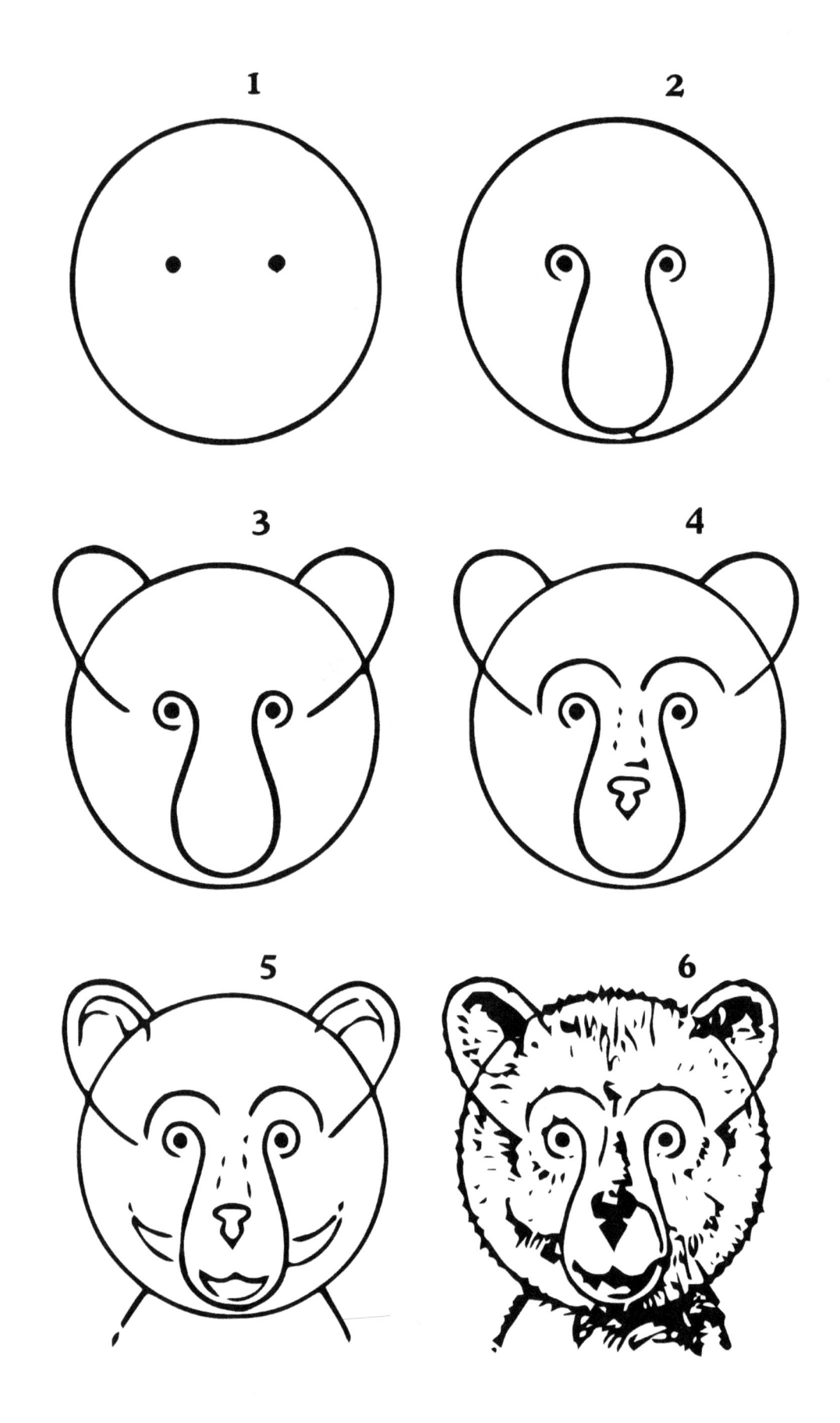

3 4

5 6

34

ASIATIC ELEPHANT

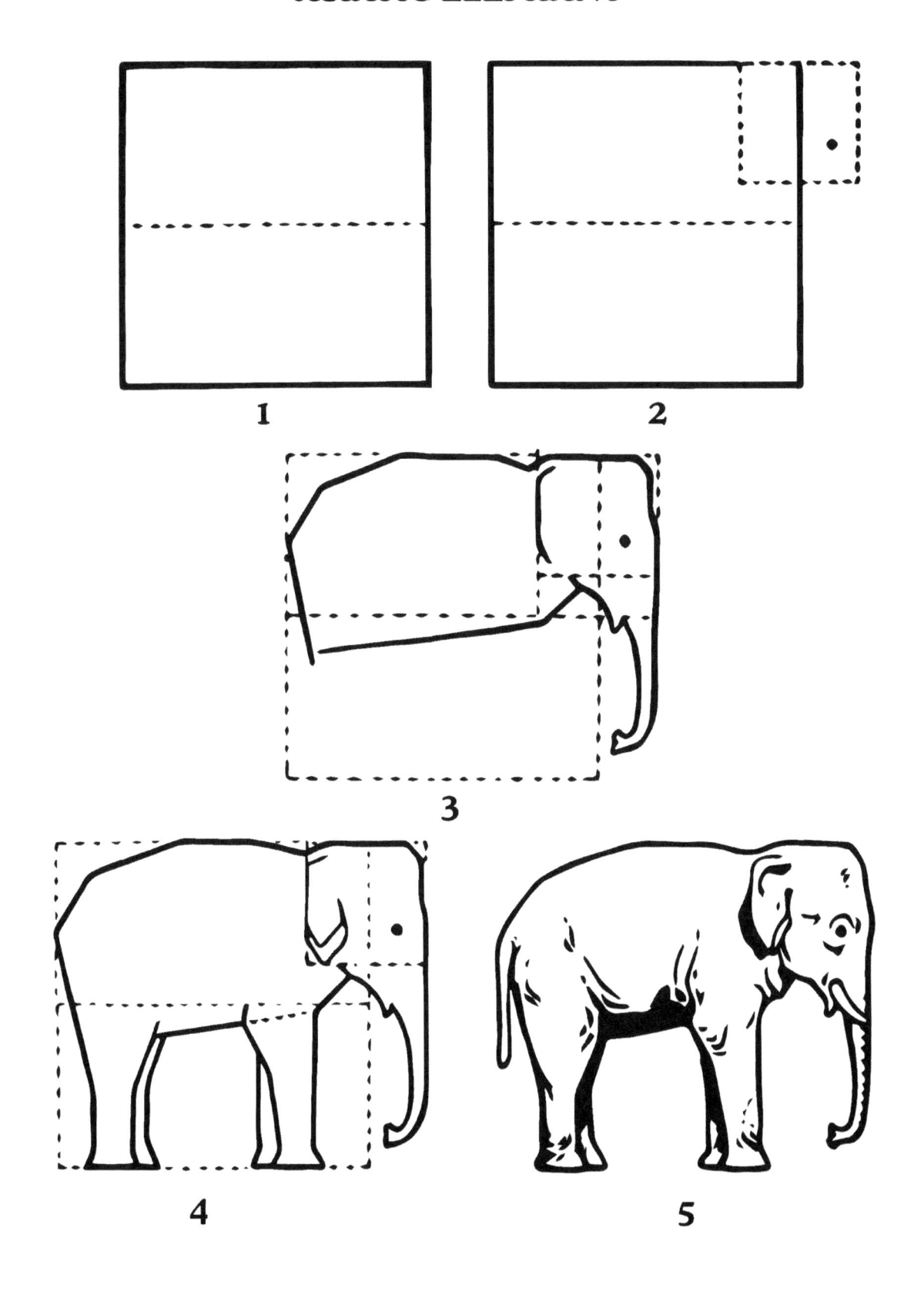

1
2
3
4
5

AFRICAN ELEPHANT

1
2
3
4
5

BABY ELEPHANTS

1 2

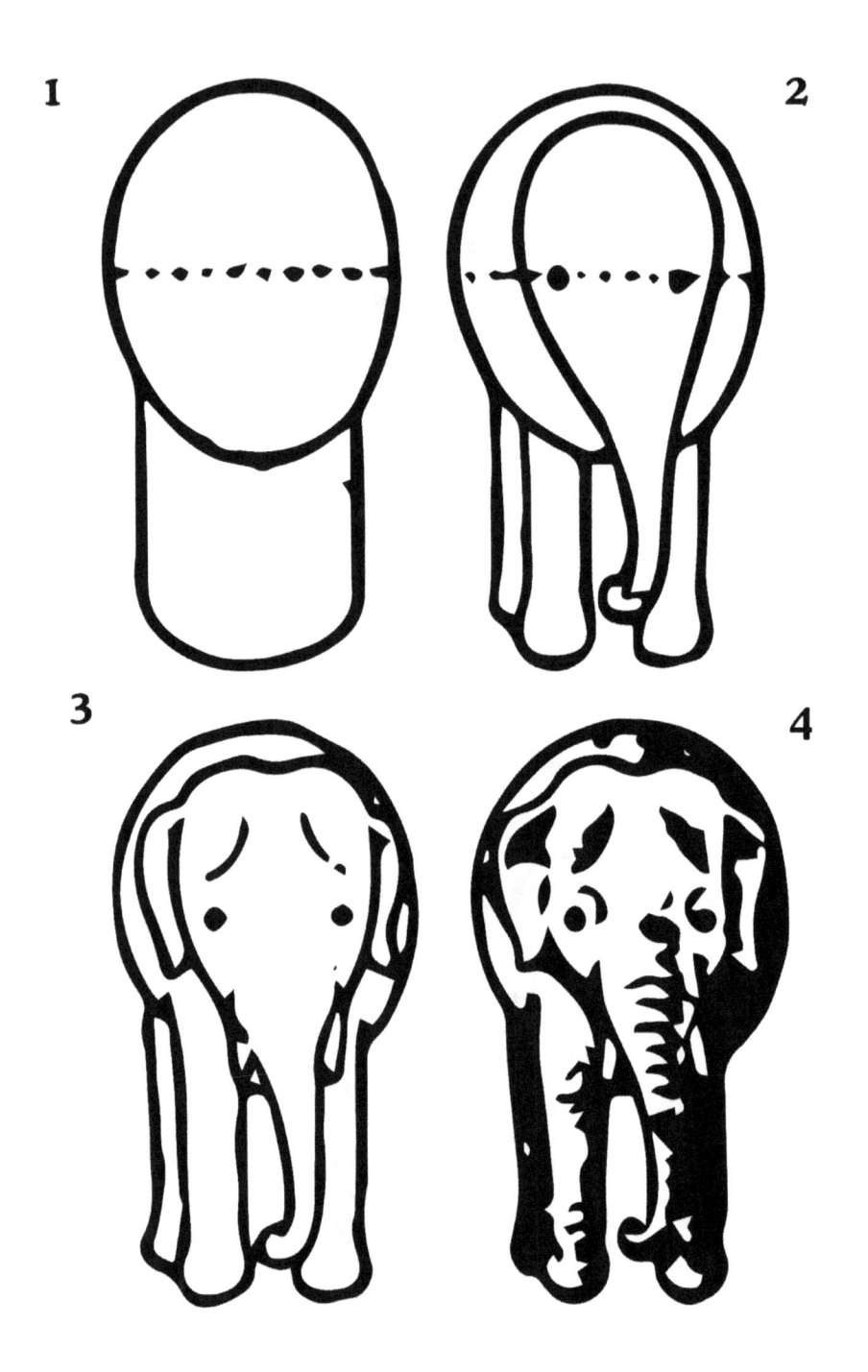

3 4

CIRCUS ELEPHANT

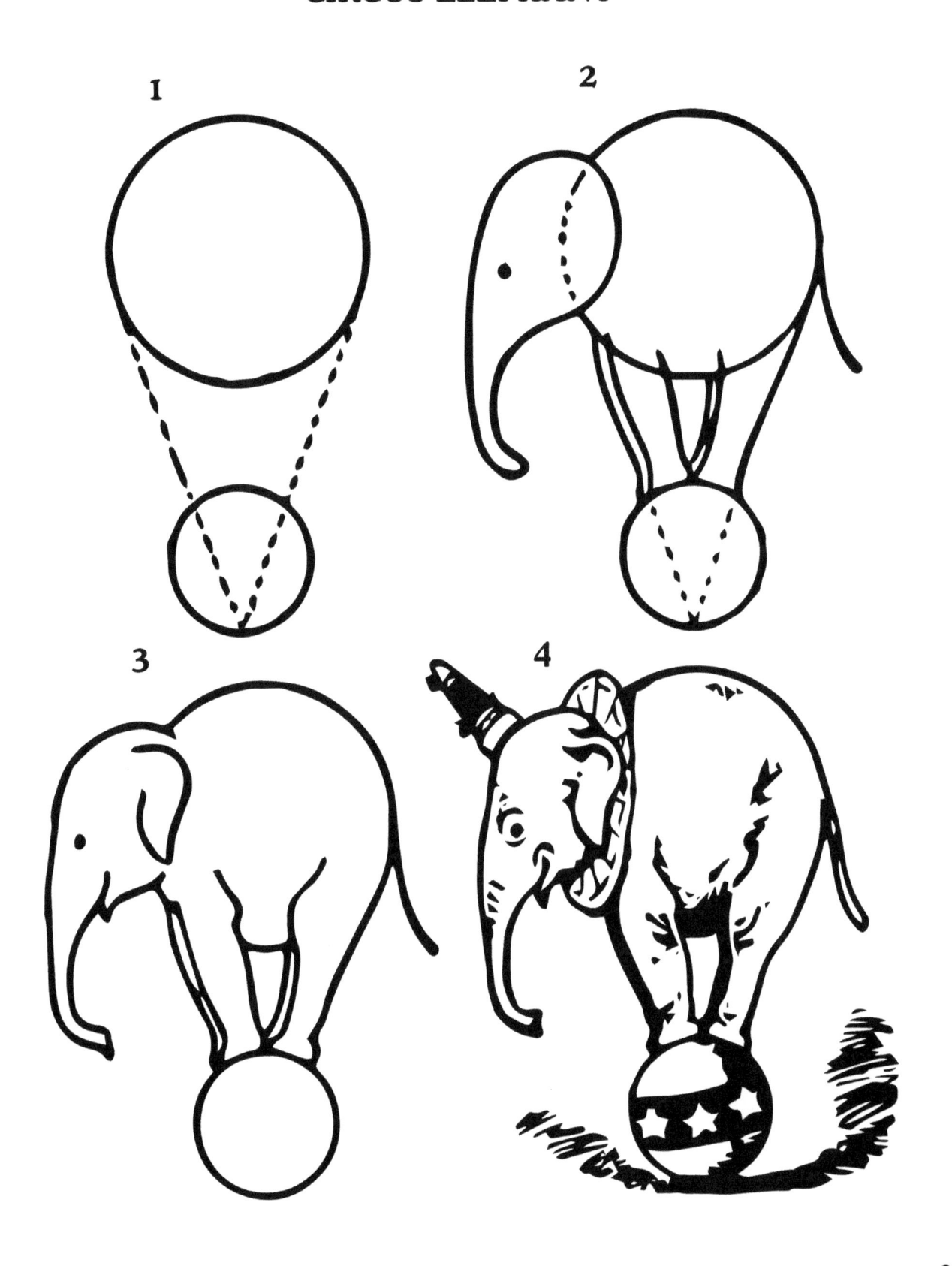

1

2

3

4

39

MONKEYS

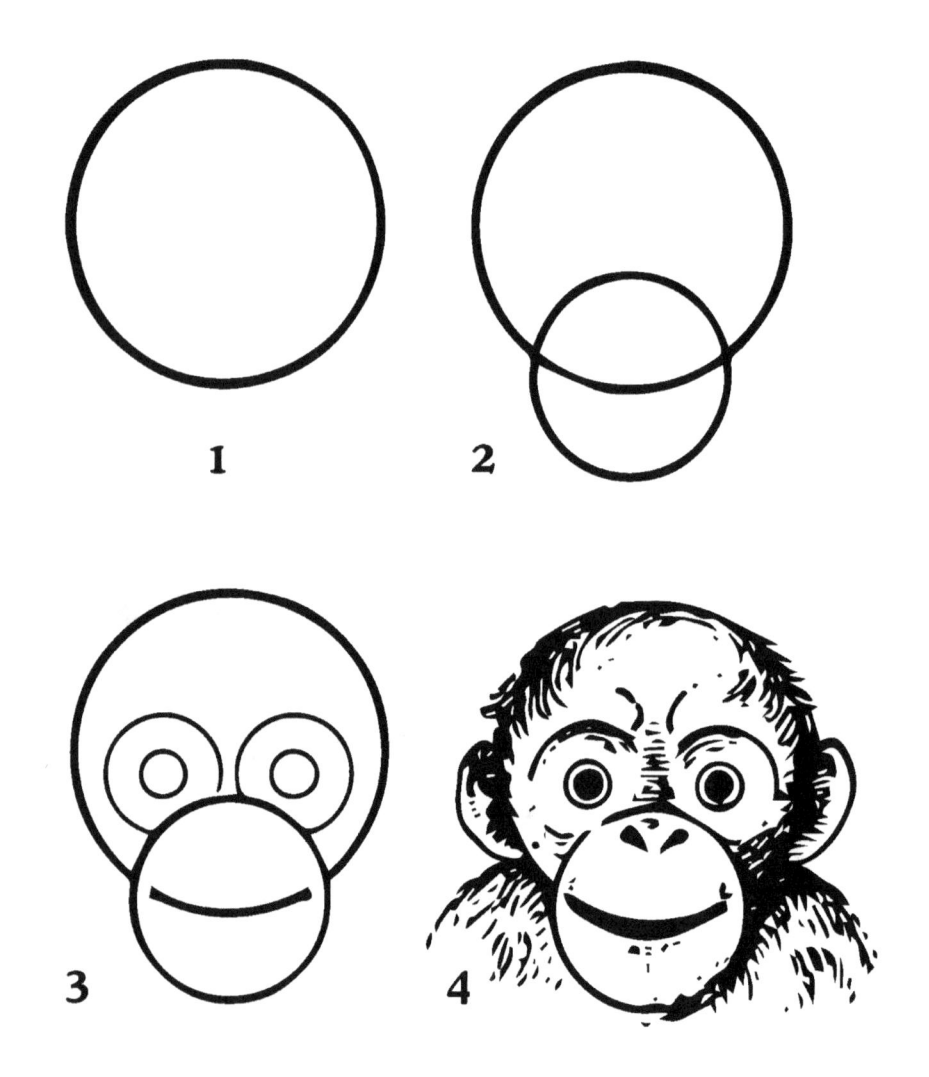

1

2

3

4

1 2 3
4 5
6 7

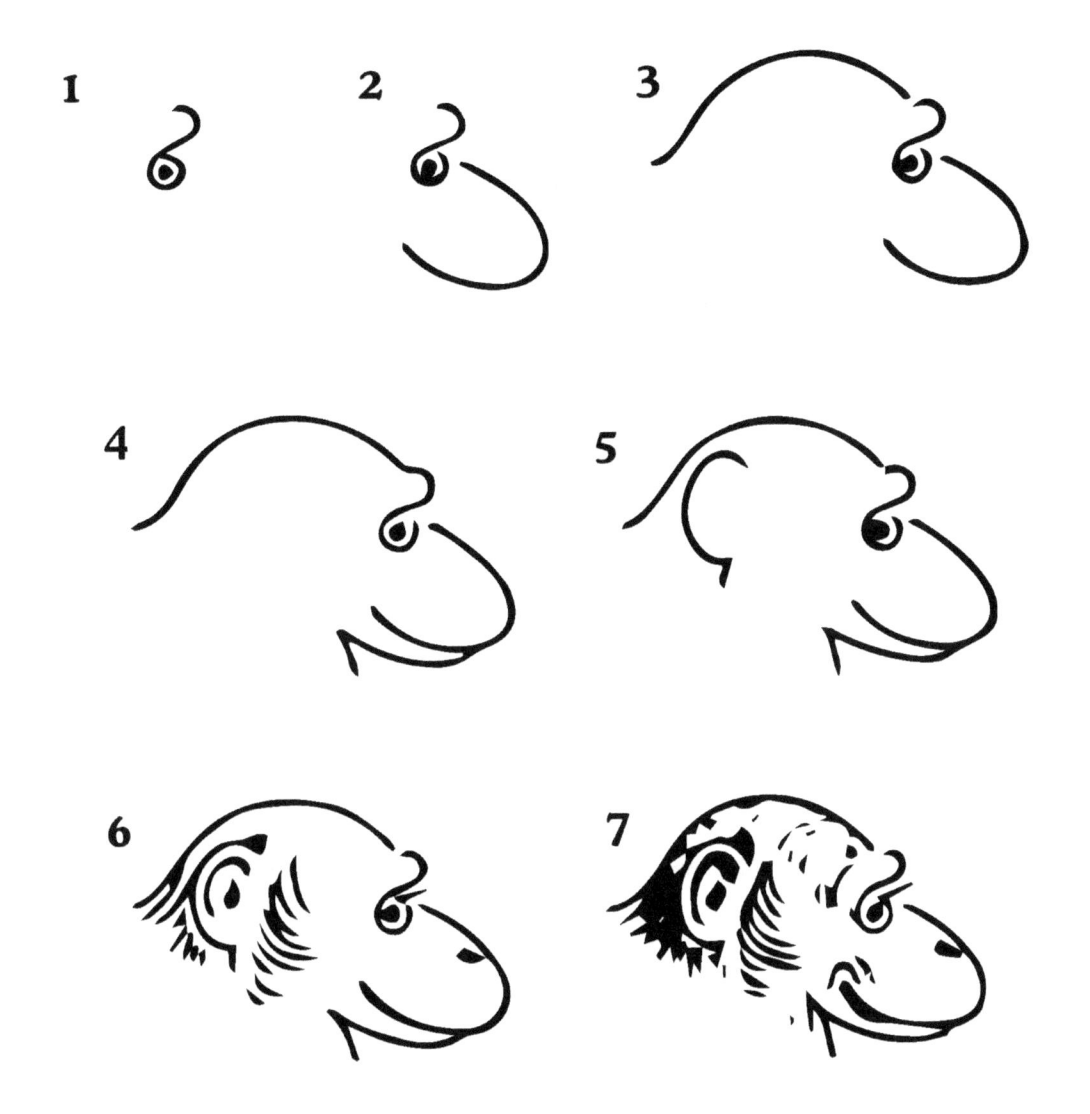

MICE

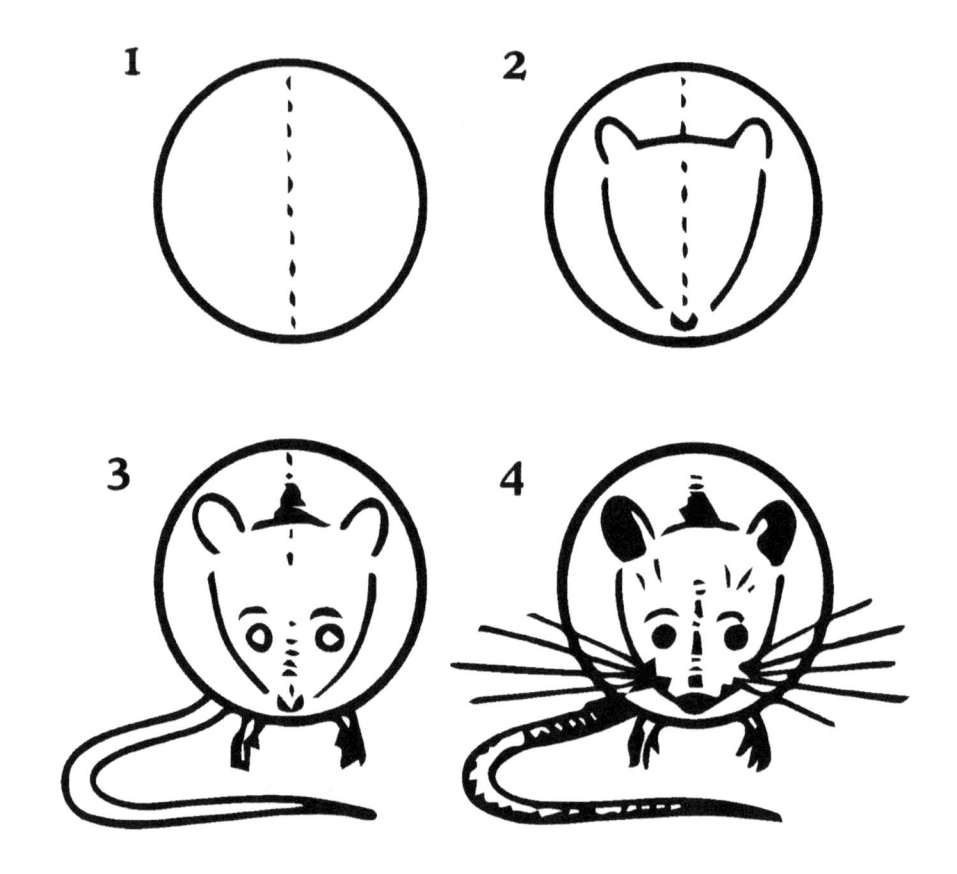

1

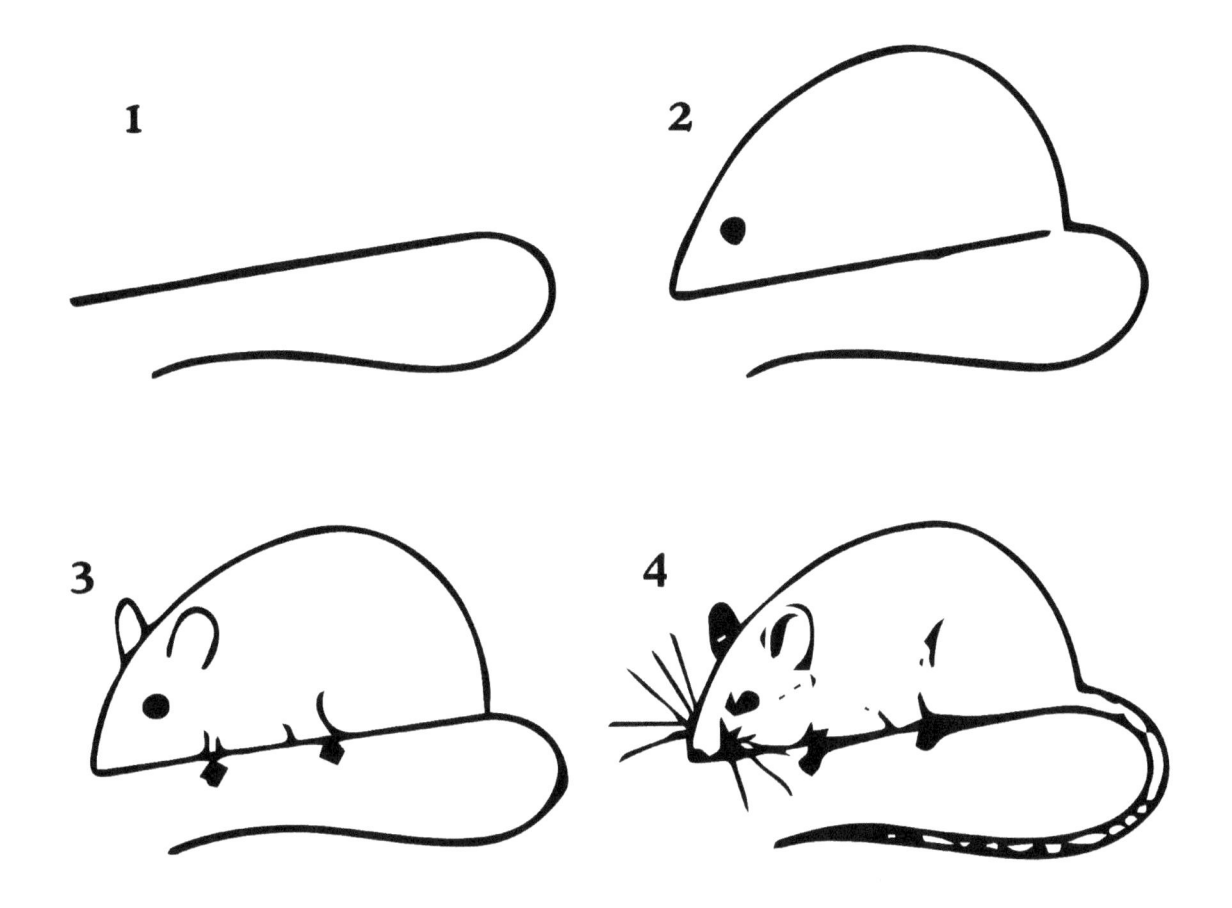

2

3

4

43

1 2

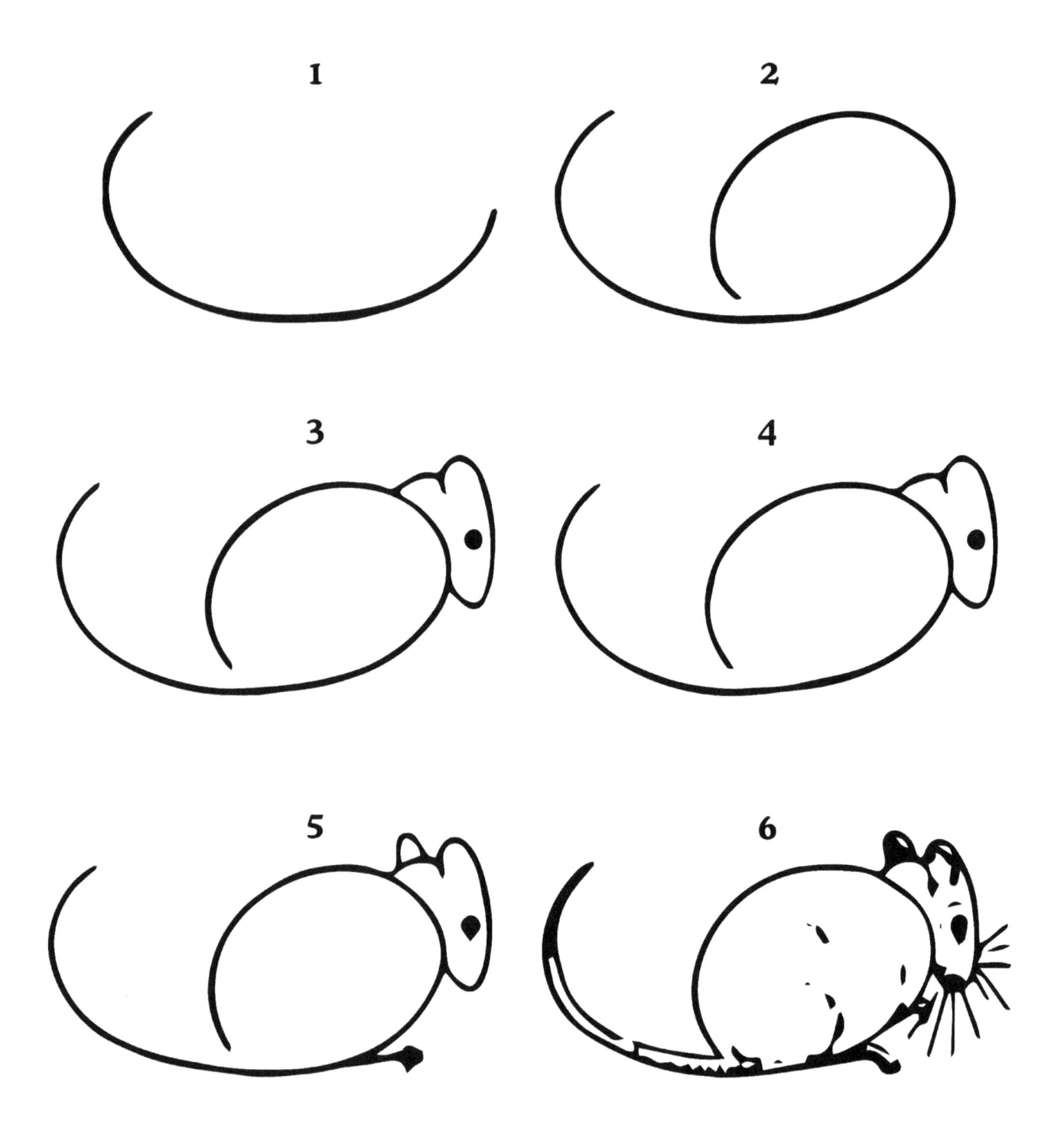

3 4

5 6

44

1

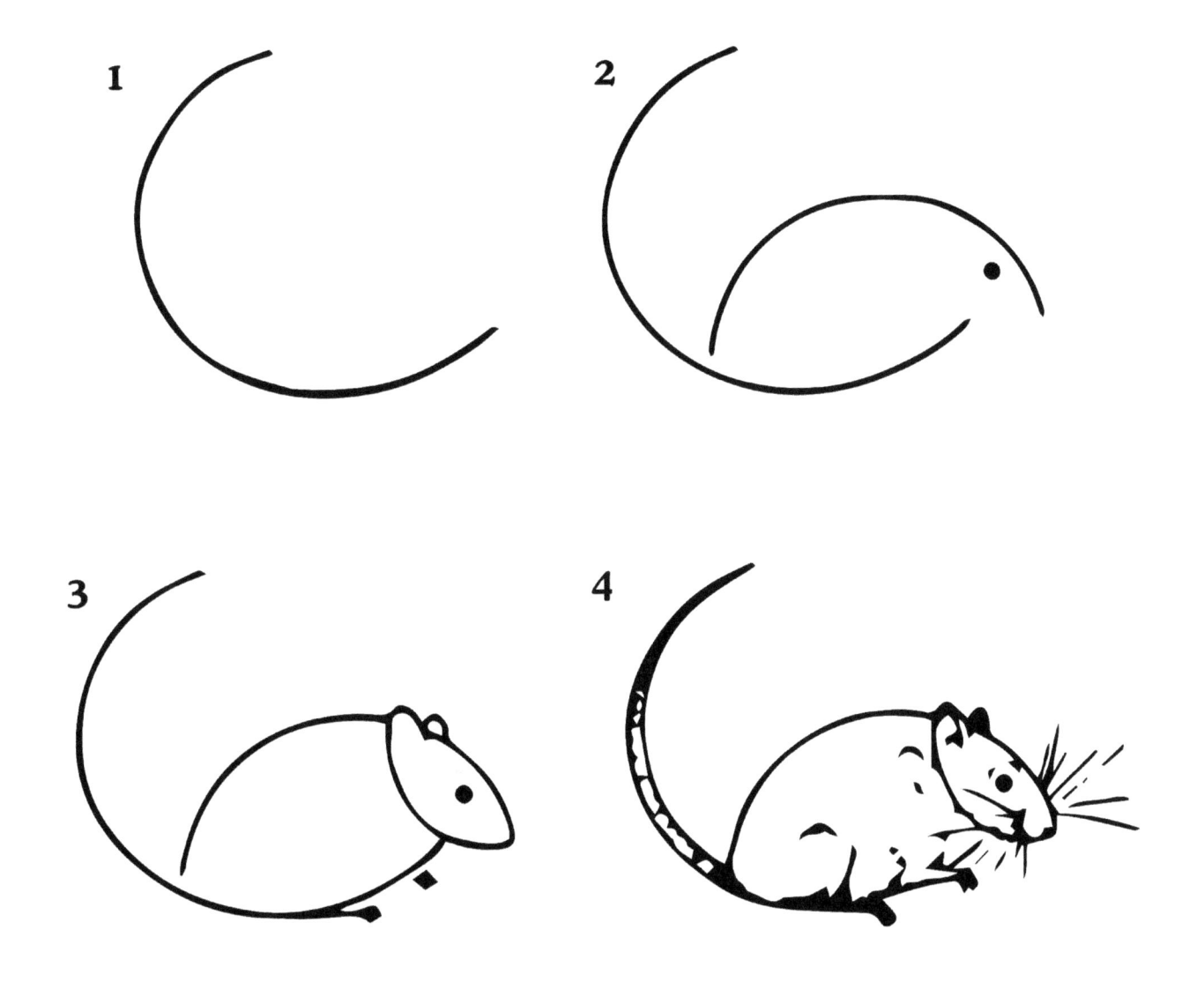

2

3

4

1

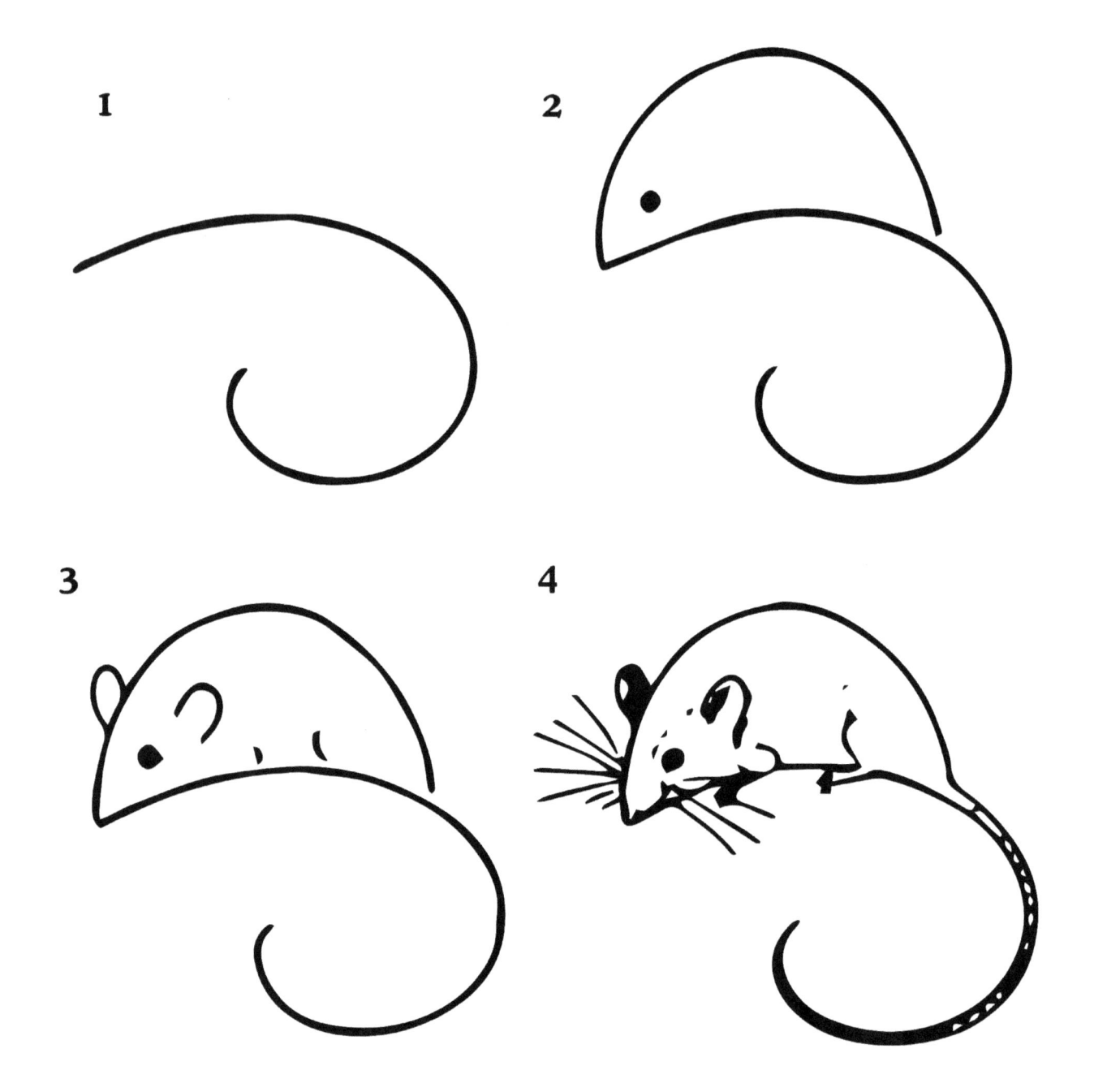

2

3

4

1

2

PRAIRIE-DOGS

The prairie-dogs really haven't very strongly defined character. Some character they have, of course, but it is merely that they are fat little bodies. The simple outlines at the top show what you are to draw first to indicate this character.

BUFFALO

The crinkly mass of the buffalo's head is rather hard to represent in lines with a lead-pencil. The proper tool would be a brush filled with color with which you could paint quickly the large mass of hair and get the outline soft and woolly, as it really is in nature. However, you will learn something by trying to do the best you can in following the lesson on the page. Afterward you may paint his picture with a brush and color.

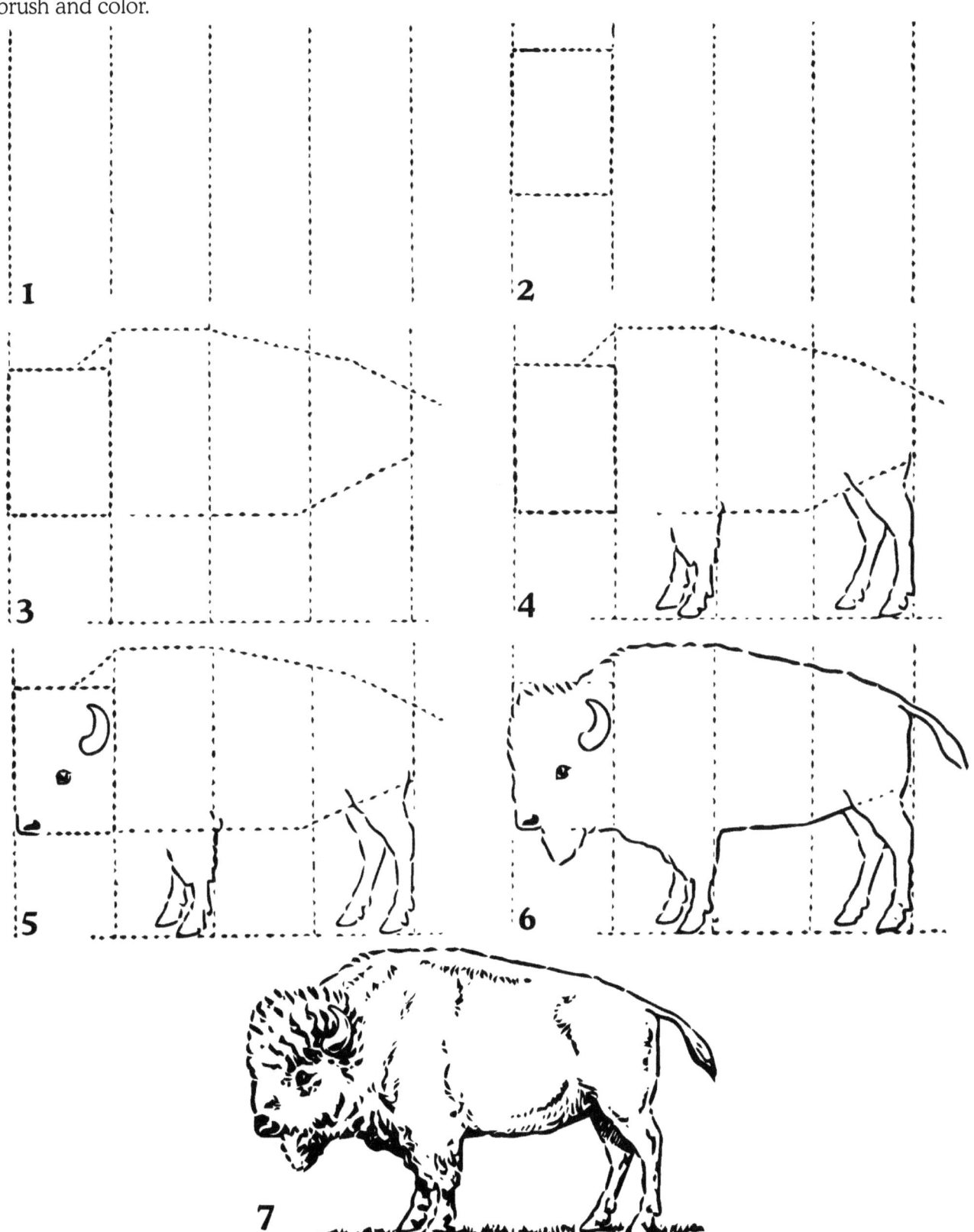

49

FOX'S HEAD

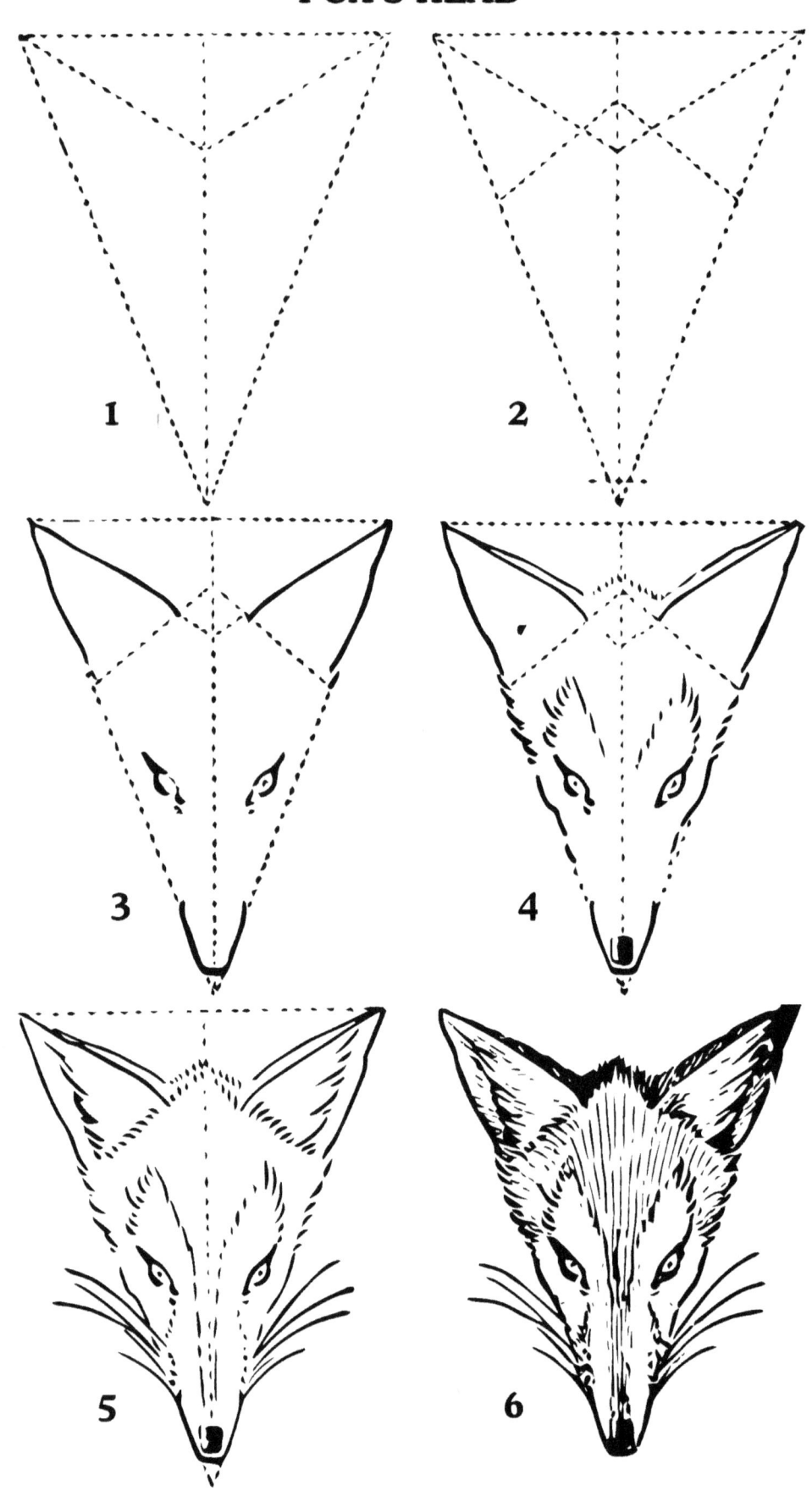

1

2

3

4

5

6

KANGAROO

GIRAFFE

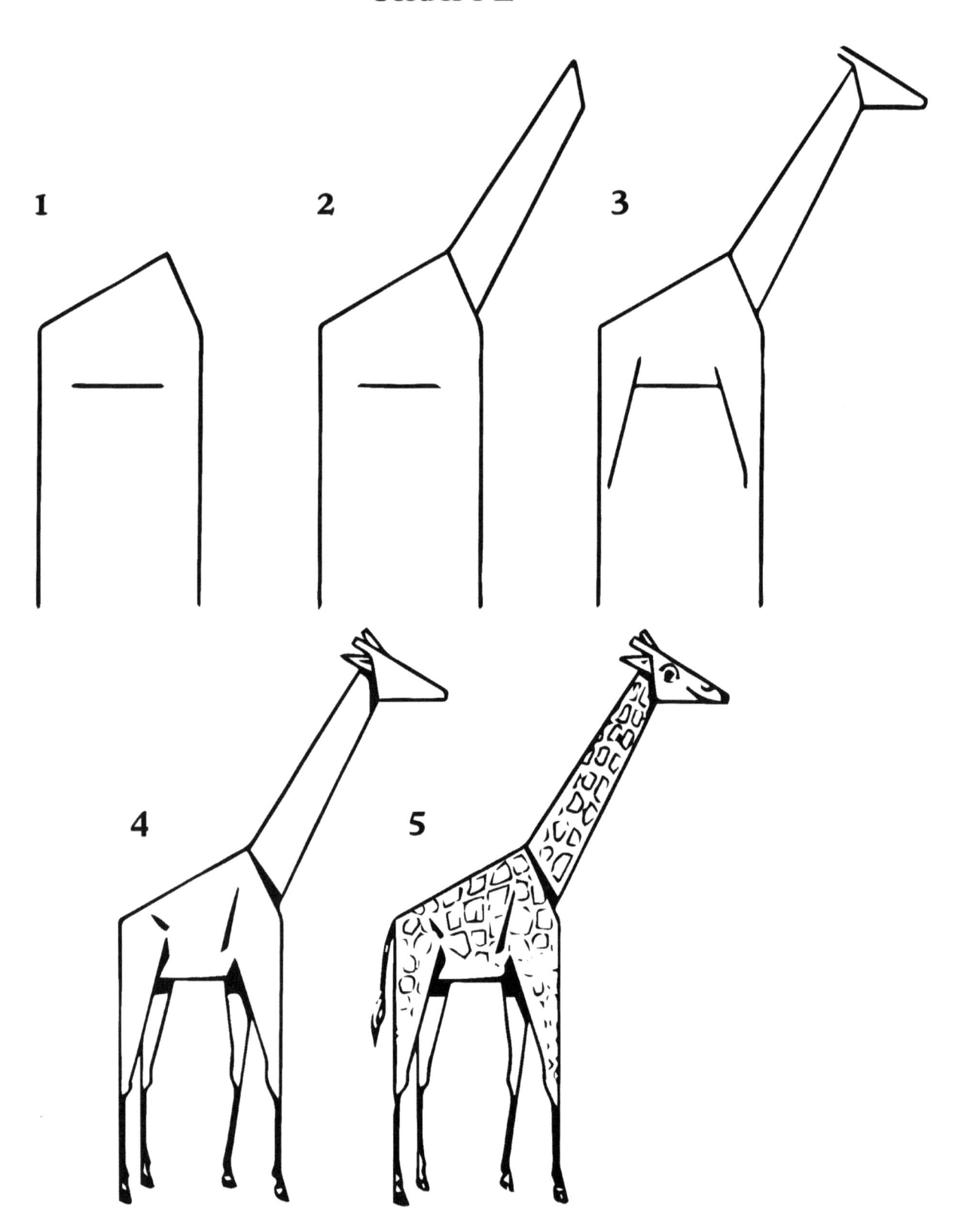

1
2
3
4
5

CAMEL

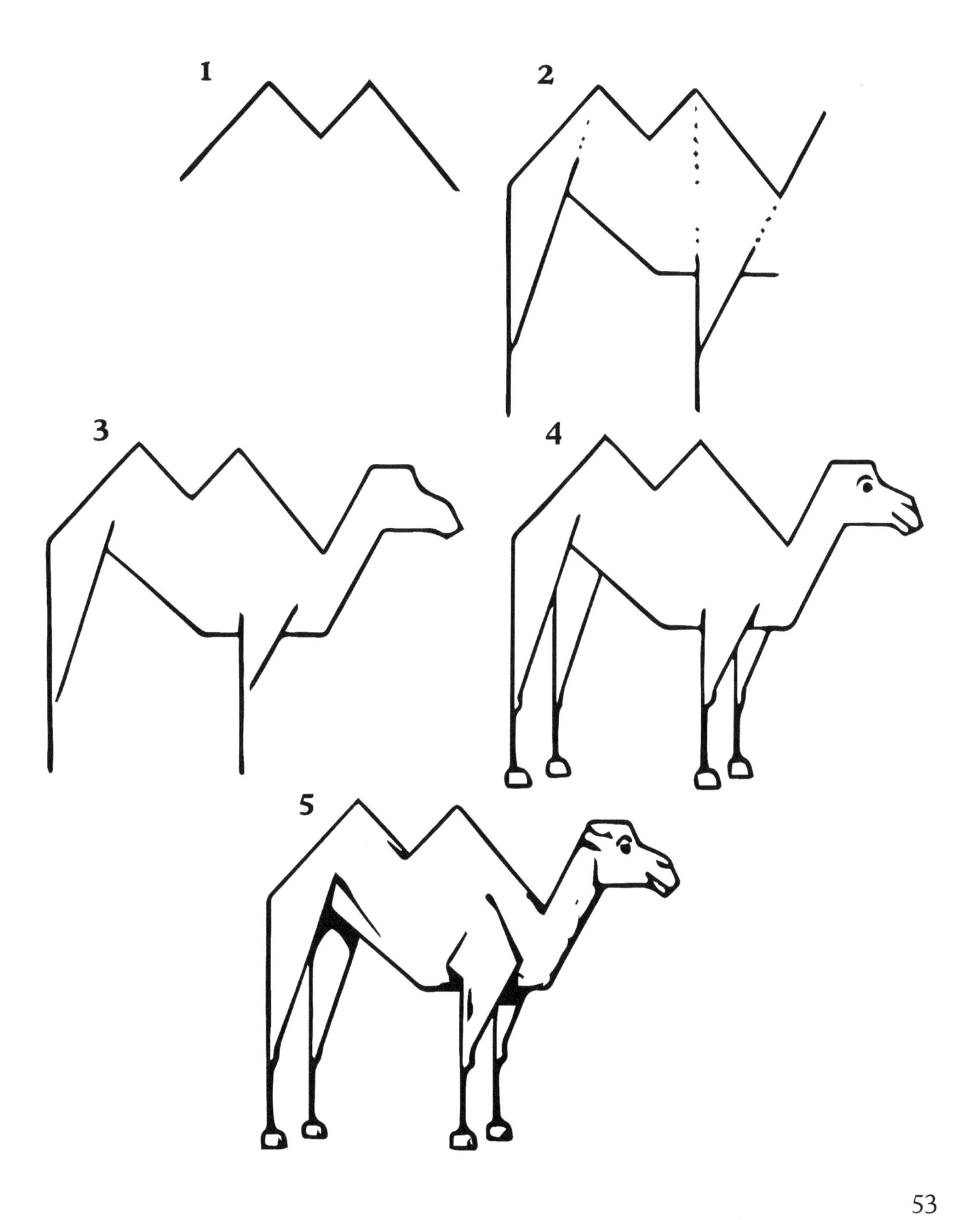

SECTION TWO
Creatures of The Air

BEES

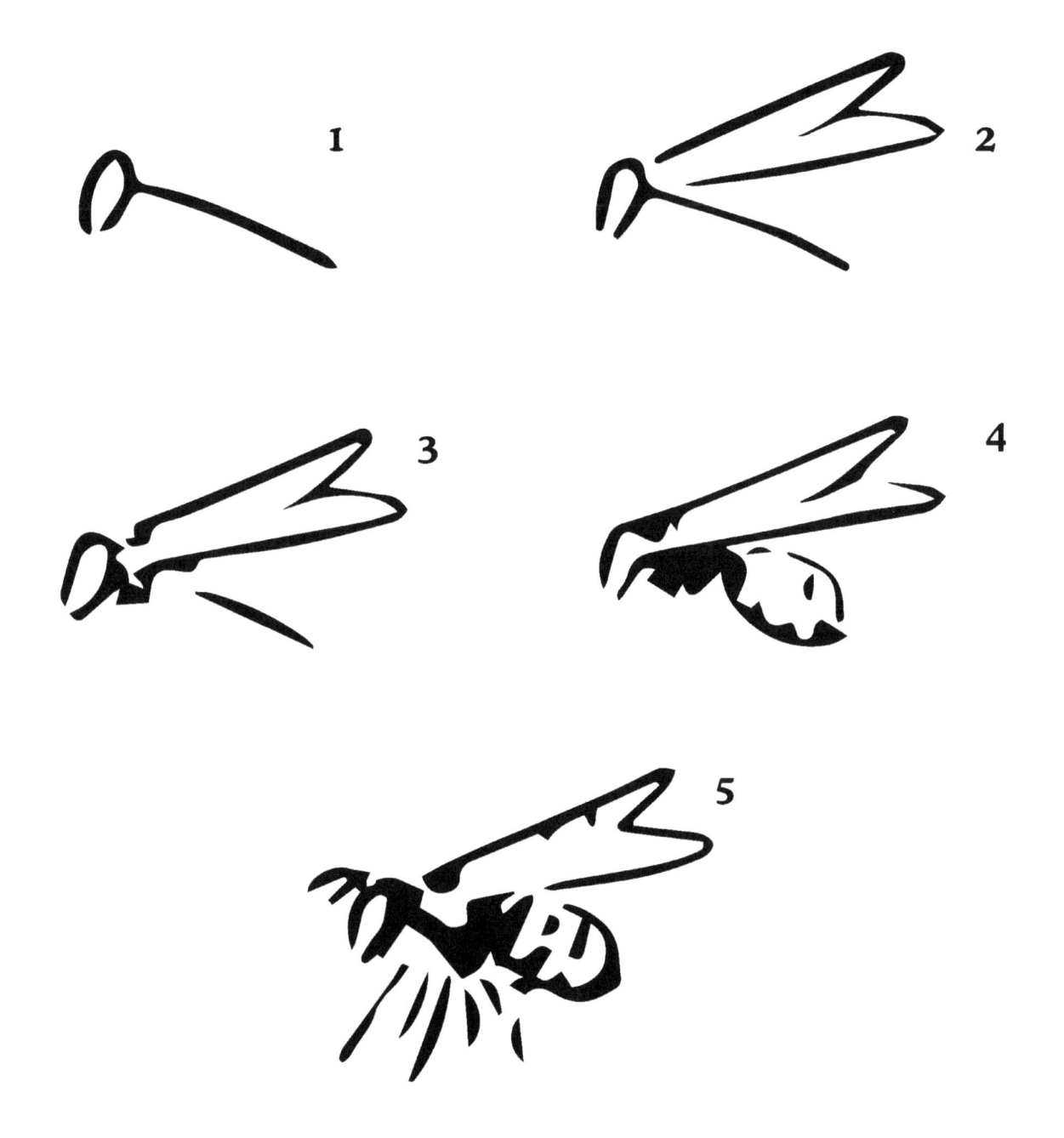

1
2
3
4
5

58

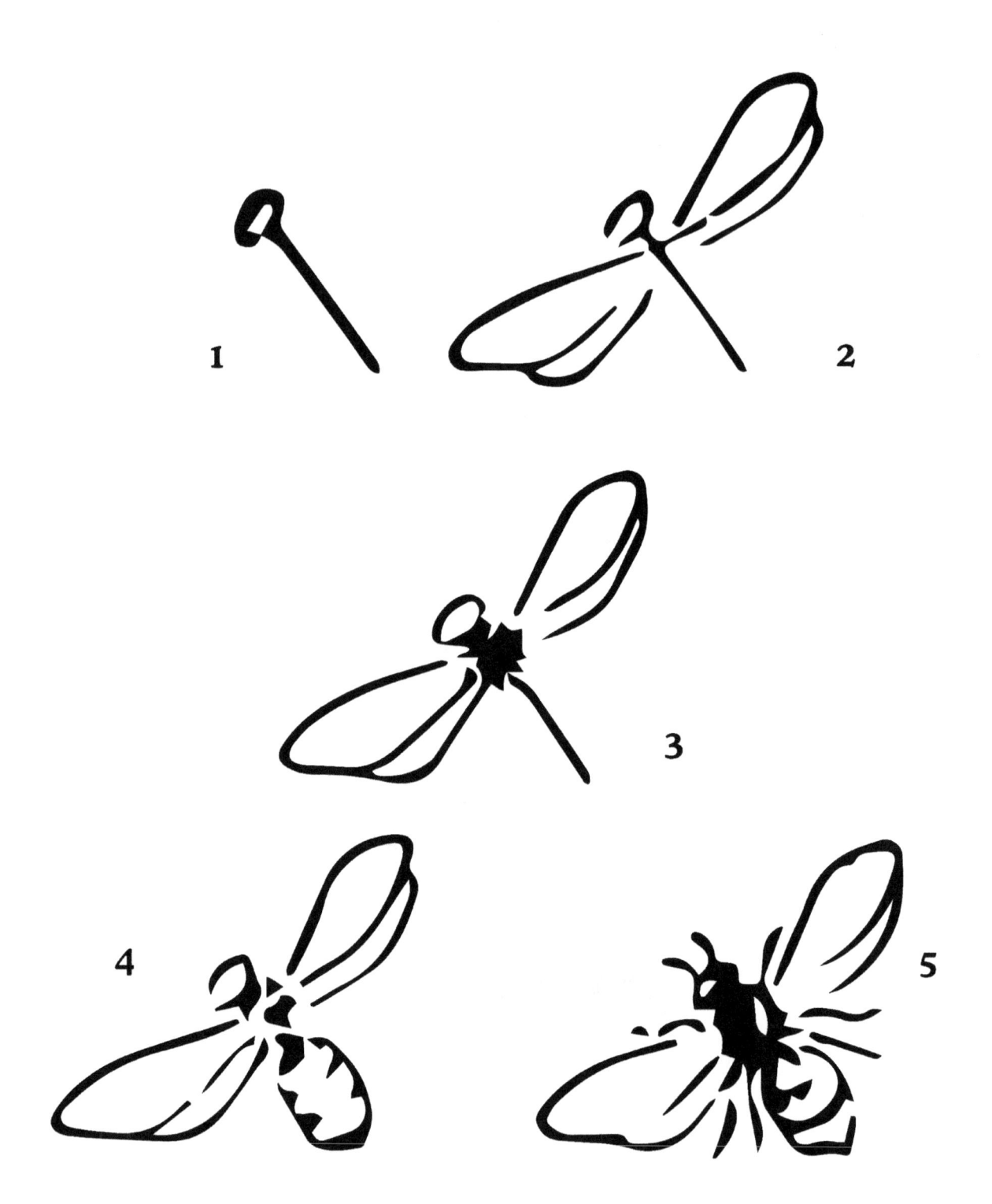

1

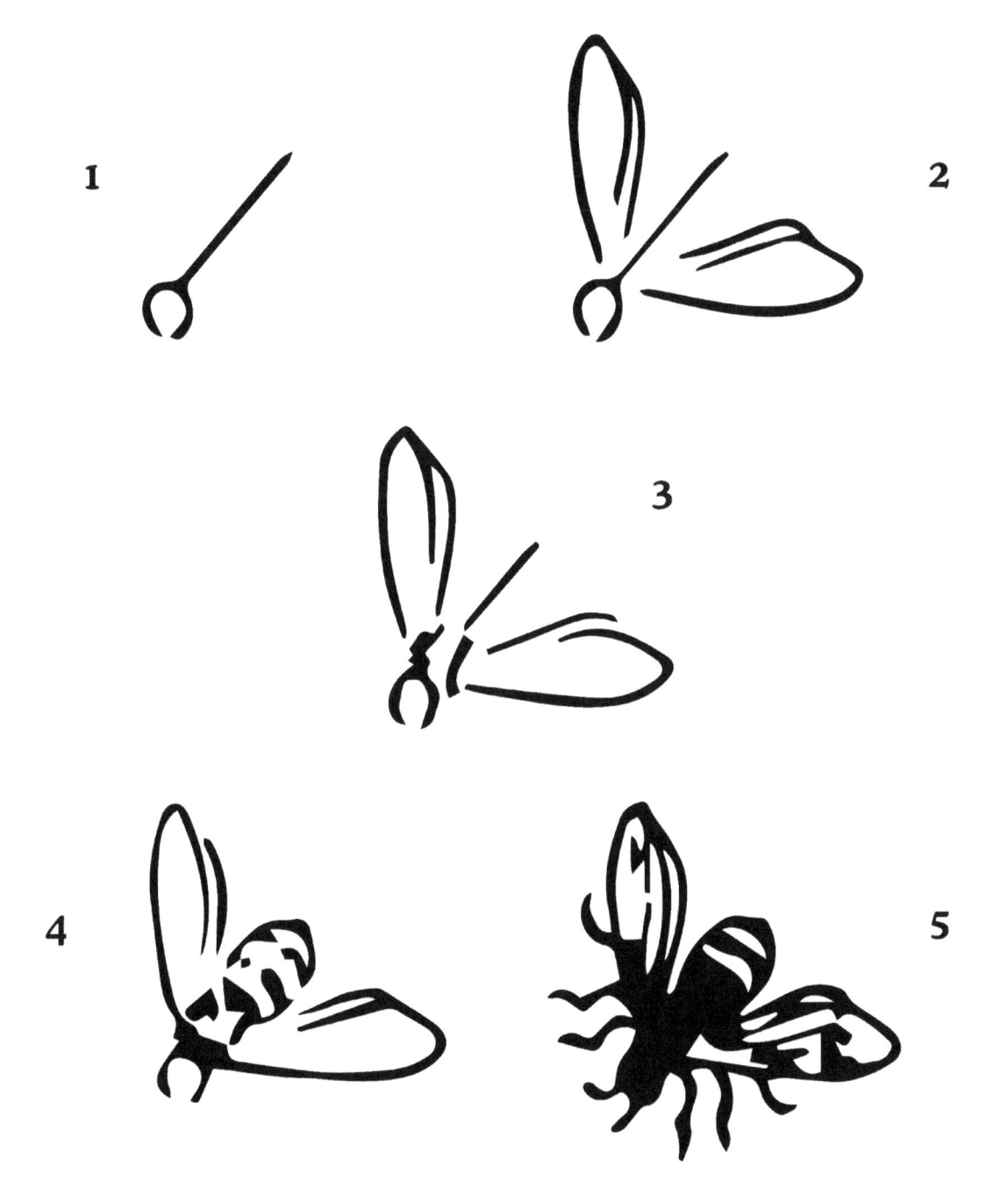

2

3

4

5

59

DRAGONFLY

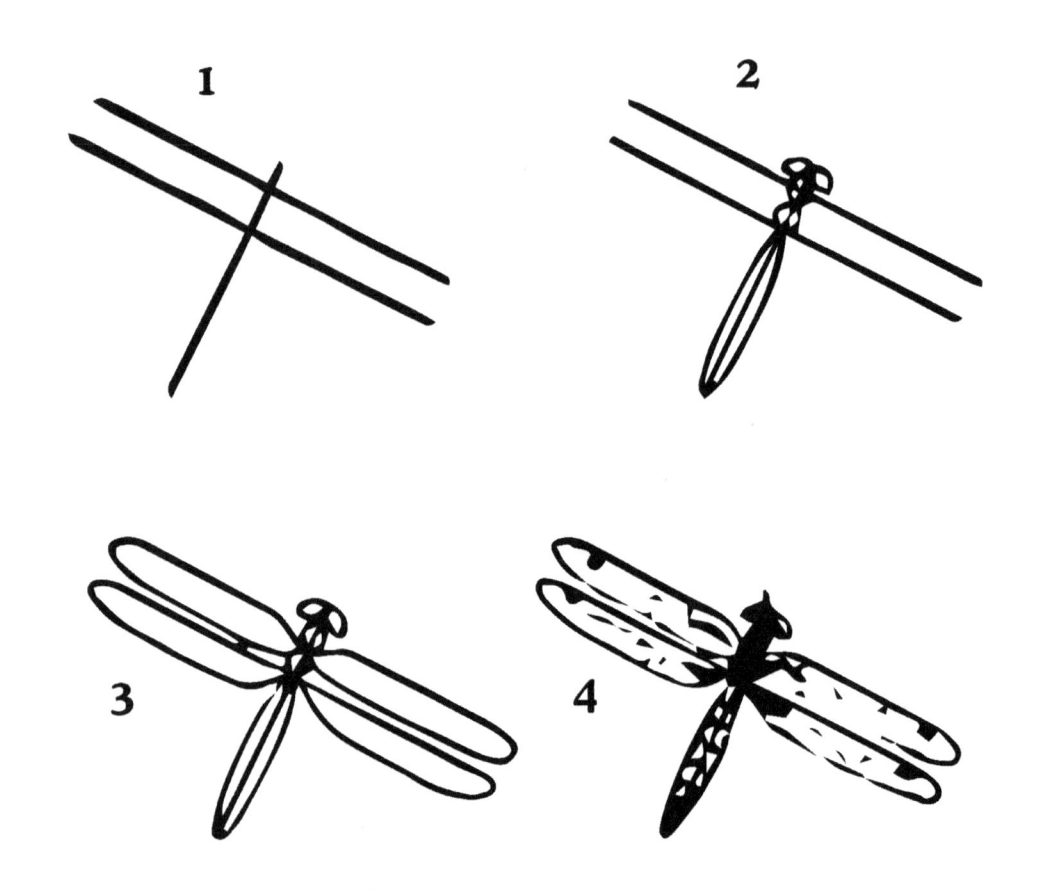

BUTTERFLIES

Making pictures of butterflies is not difficult. You will see on the following pages the progressive steps by which five different kinds are pictured. In each case it is the last figure of each series of diagrams that you are striving to copy. And Figure 1, in each case, shows the first lines that you put on the paper. The five simple combinations of lines are so expressive of our subjects, that marking them first makes a very good way to start picturing the five butterflies. Notice how one of these butterflies, in its construction lines, resembles the letter Y, while two others suggest the letter X.

61

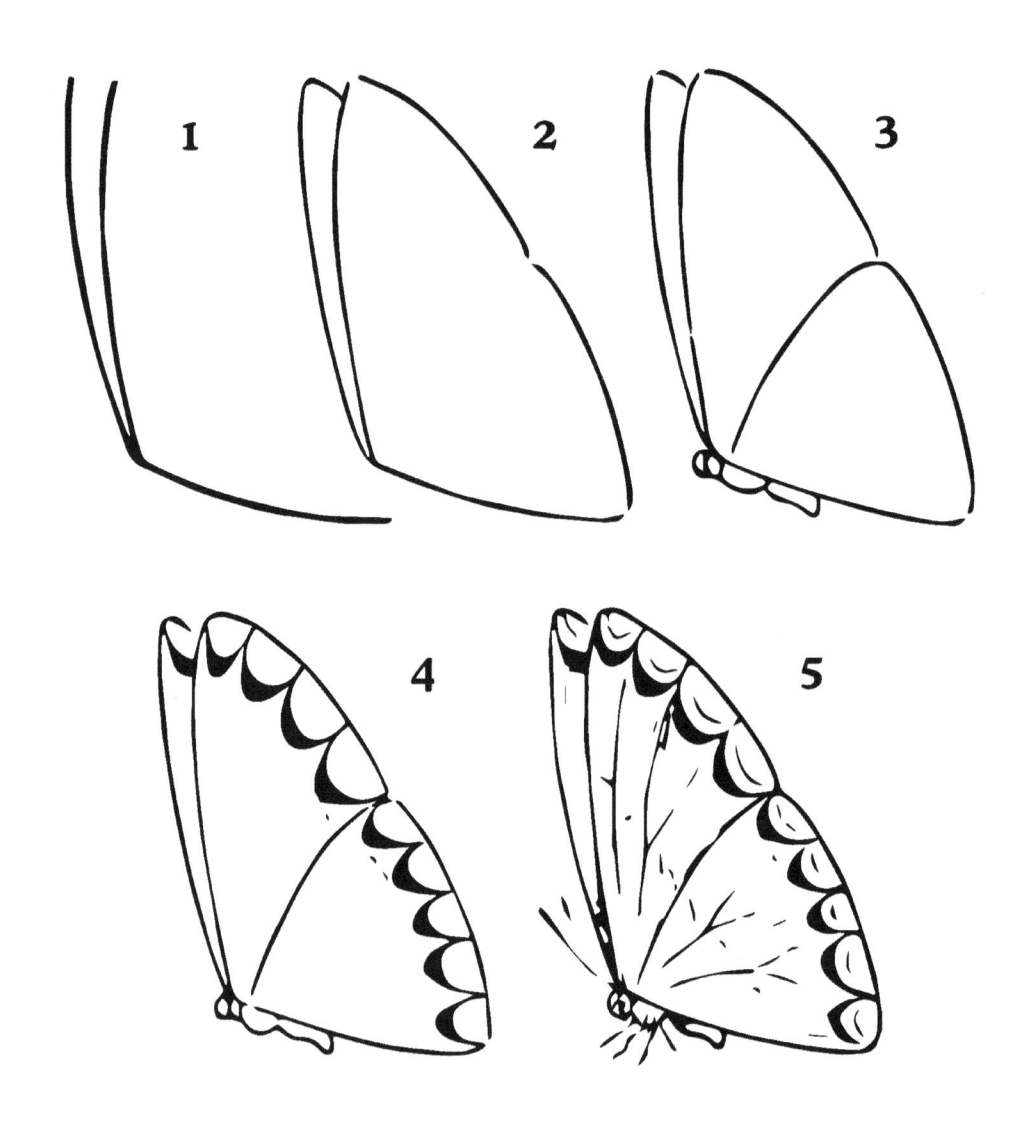

1 2 3

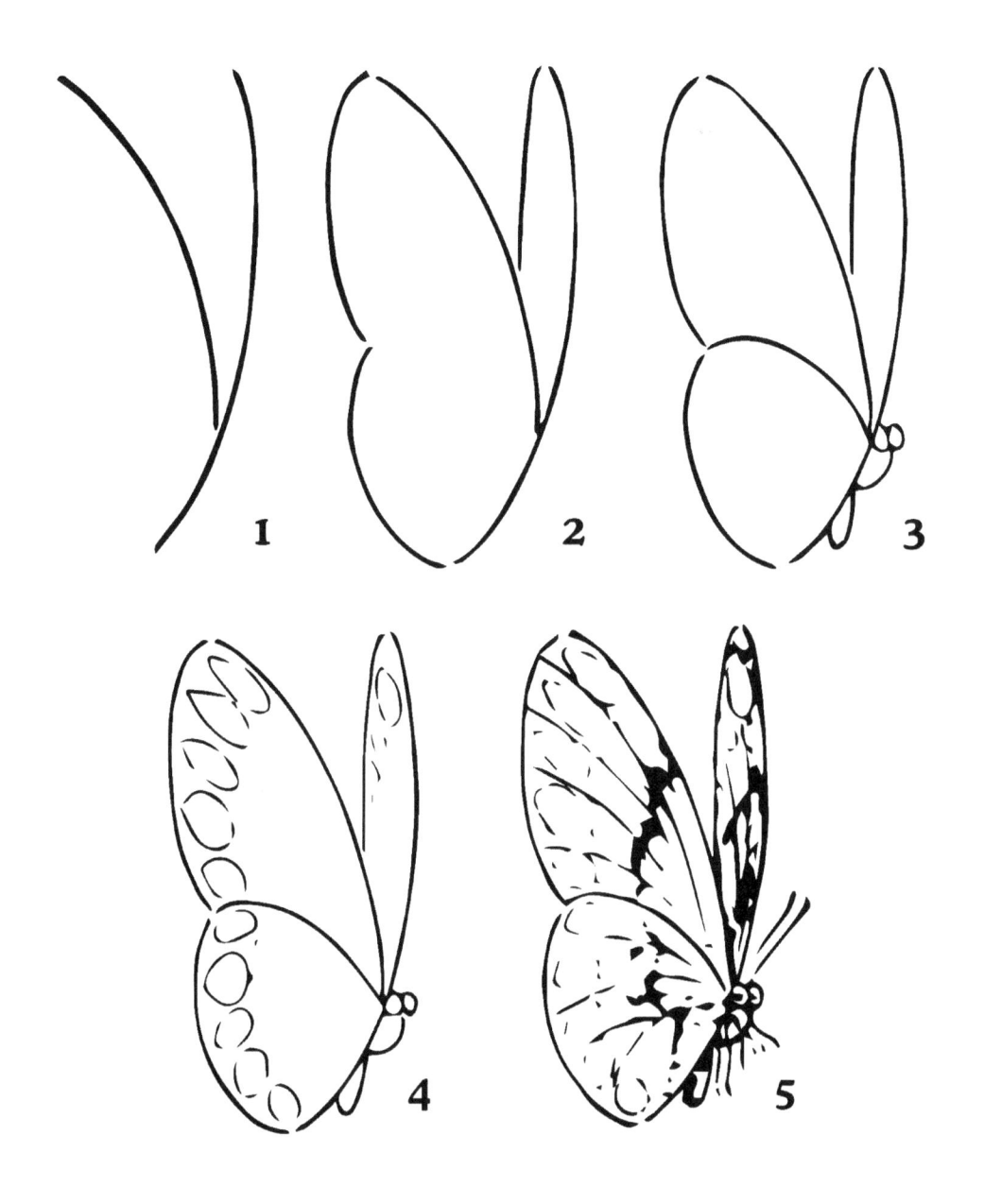

4 5

63

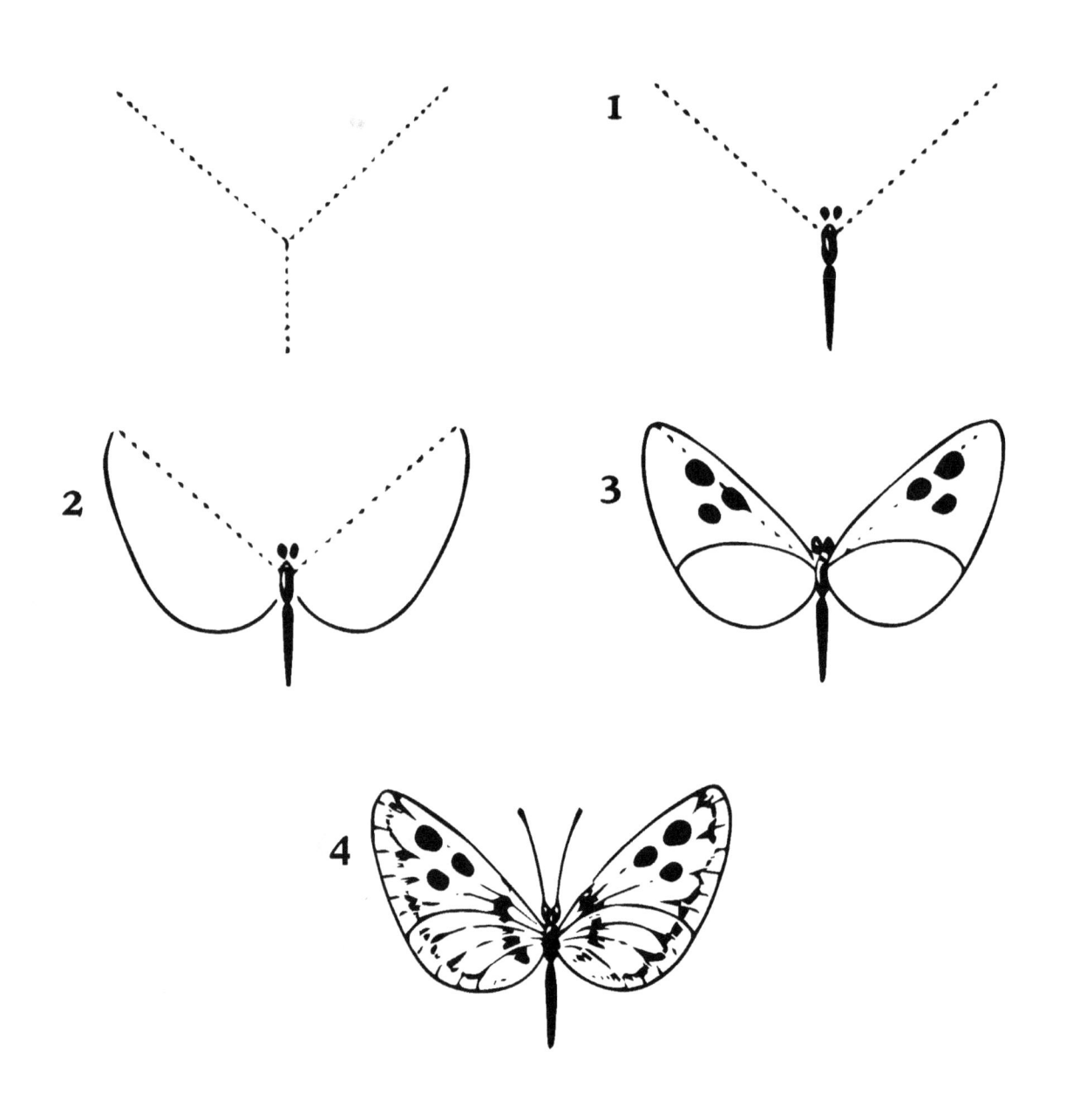

65

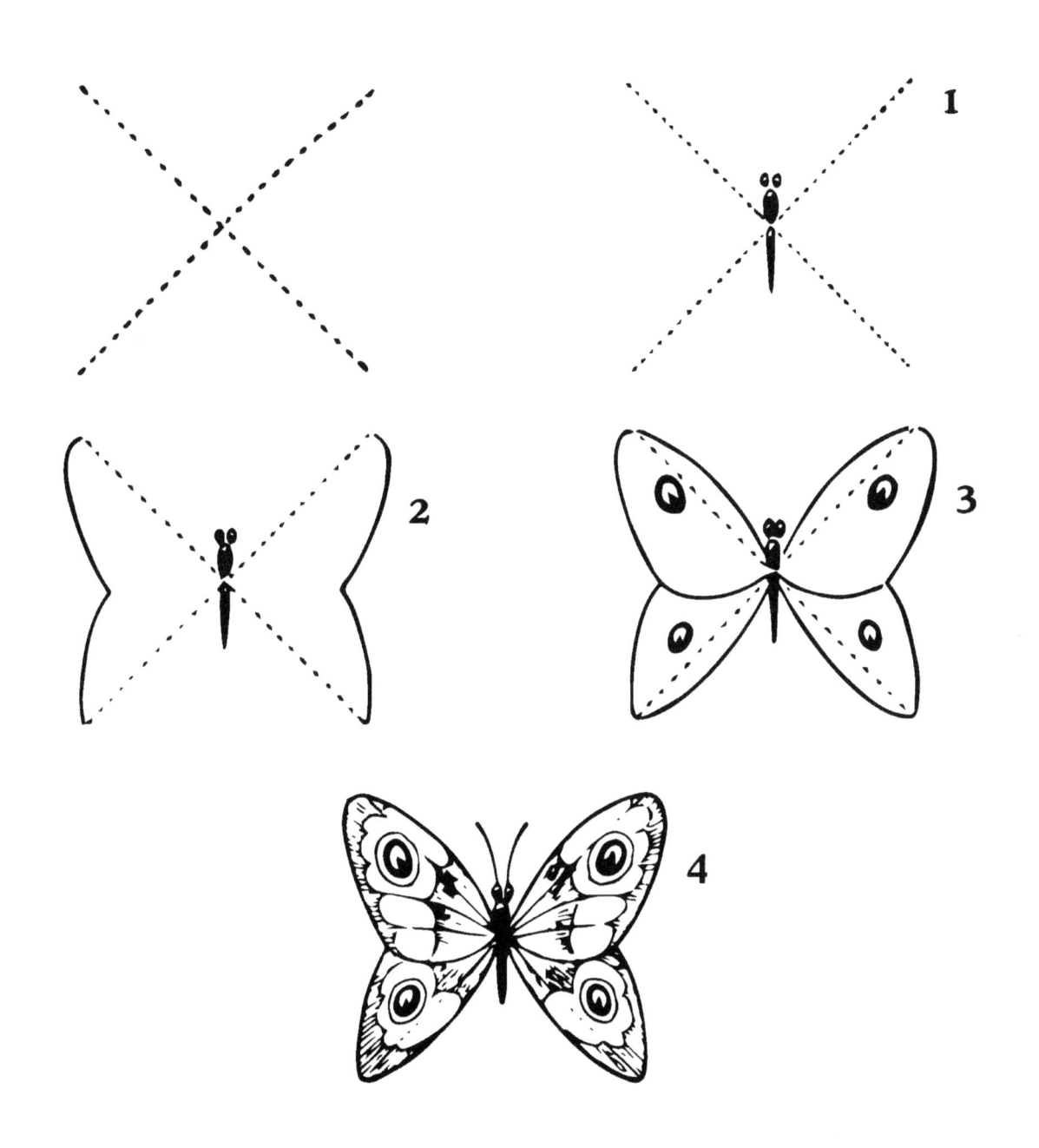

ROOSTER

1
2
3
4
5

CHICKS

1 2 3

4 5

67

1   2   3

4   5

68

HEN

DUCKS

1

2

71

1

2

72

1

2

1

2

1

2

3

4

5

1 2 3

4 5

6

GEESE

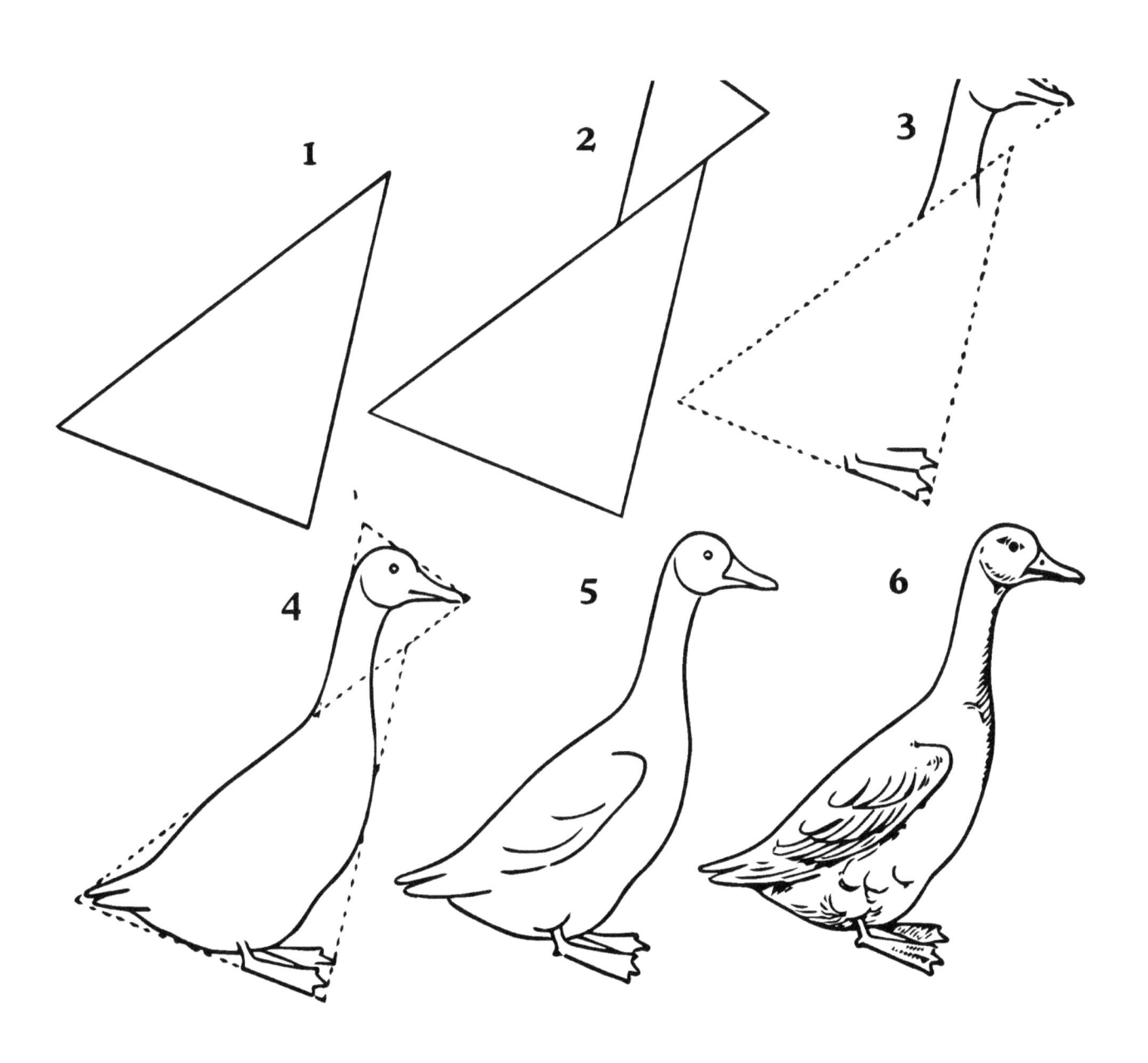

78

GOOSLING

1 2 3

4 5

OWLS

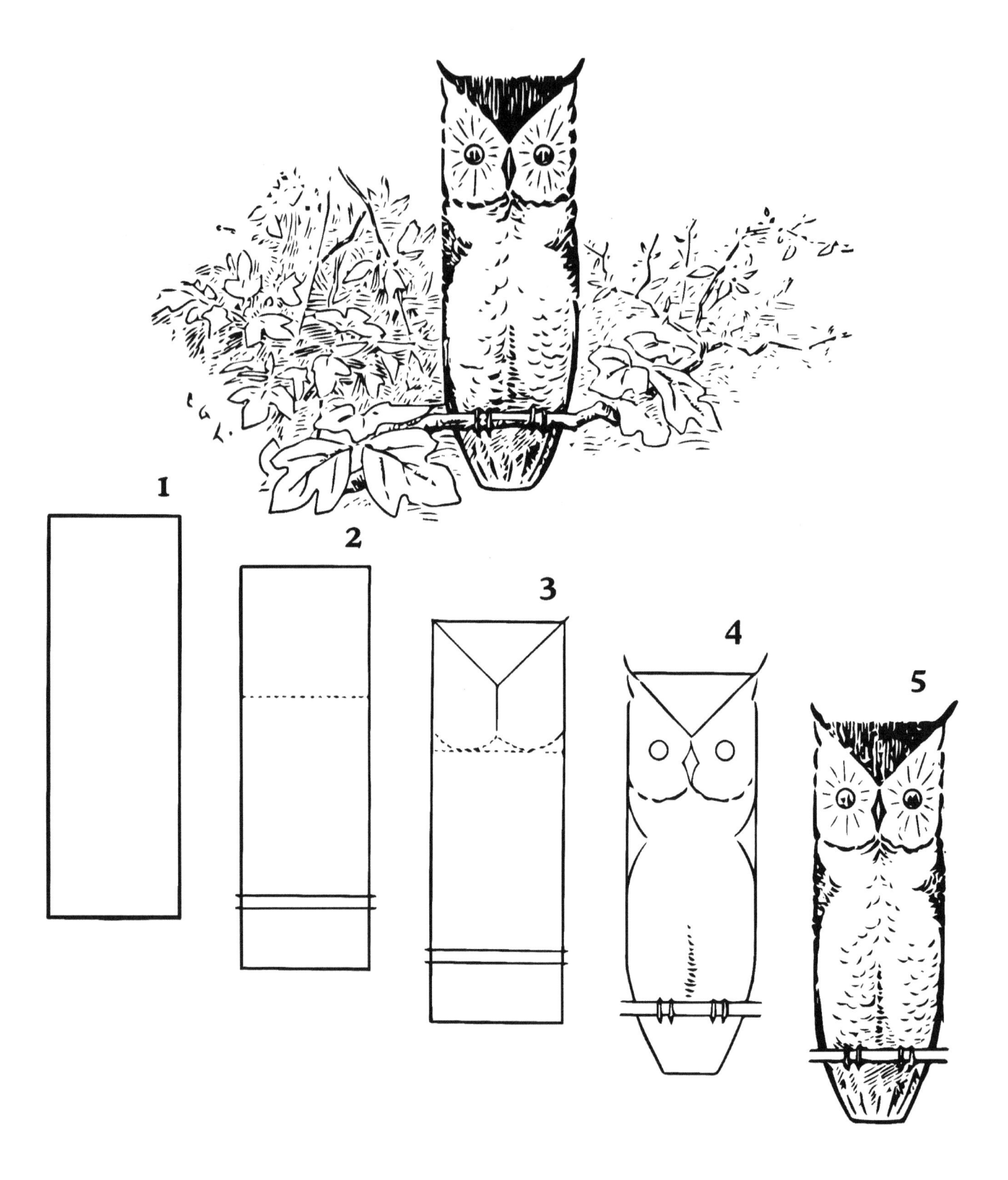

1   2   3

4   5   6

1 2 3

4 5 6

1 2 3

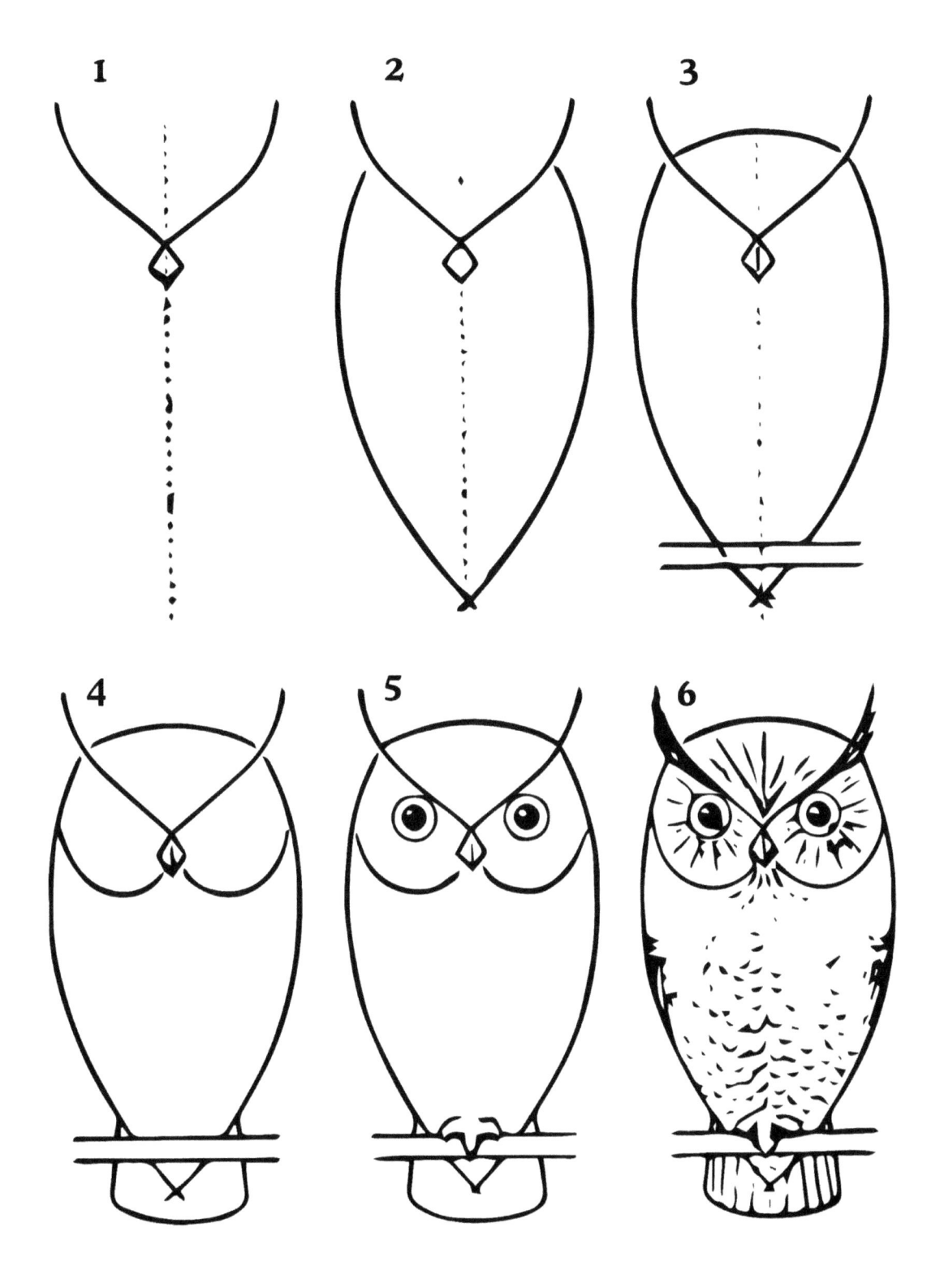

4 5 6

83

OWL'S HEAD

1
2
3
4
5

85

BOB WHITE

PARAKEETS

1 2 3
4 5 6
7 8

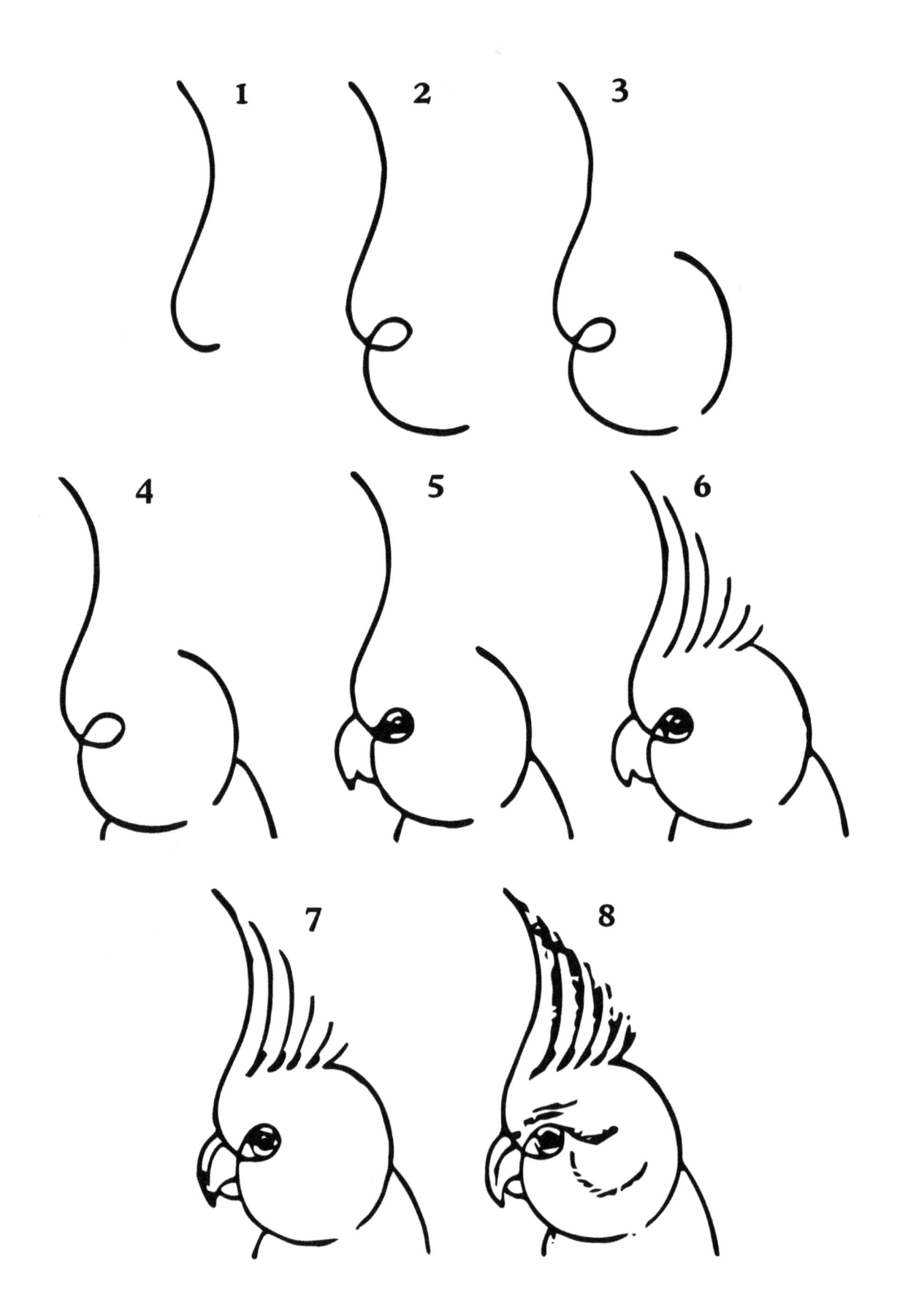

1 2

3 4

5 6

89

PARROTS

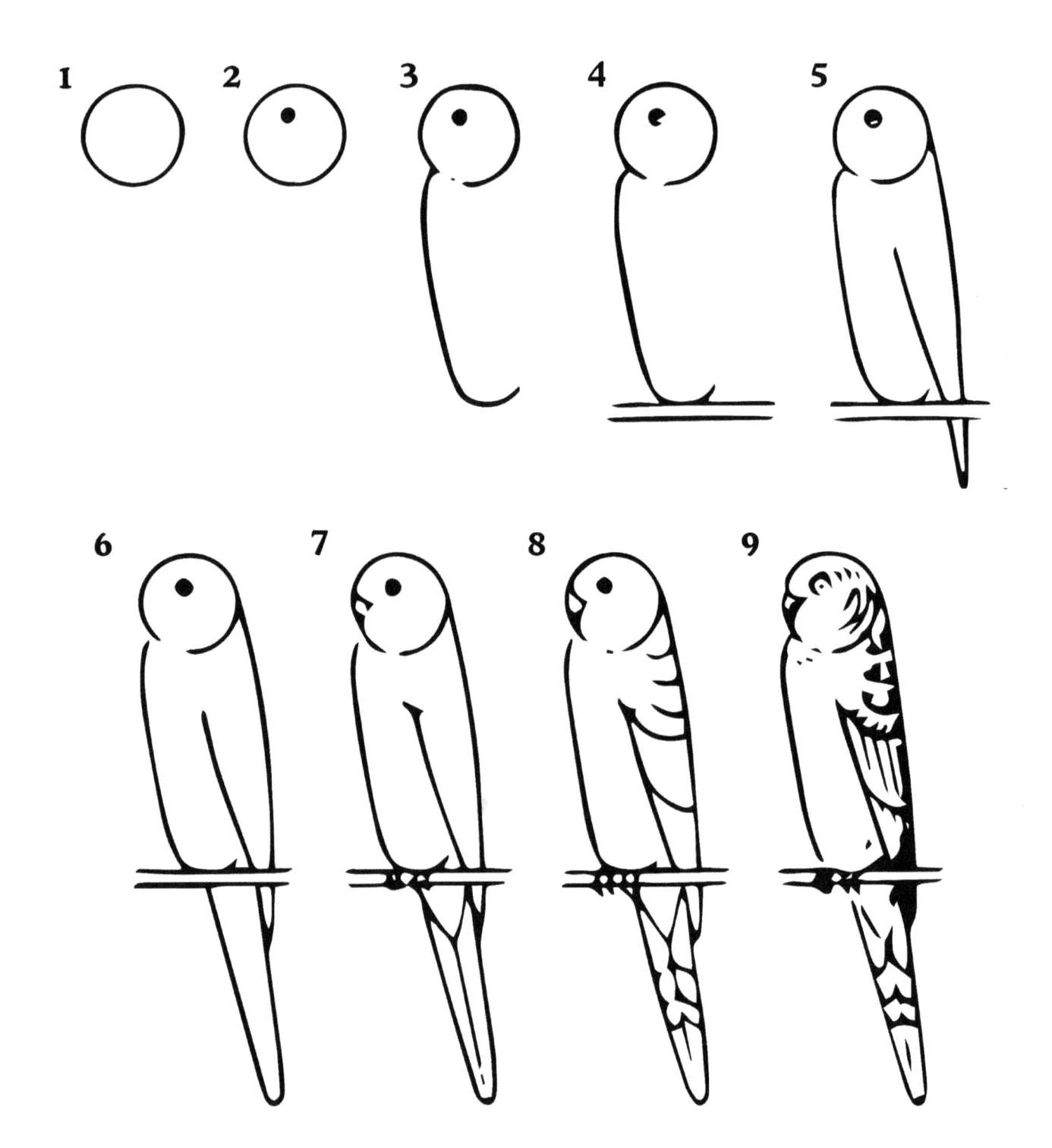

1
2
3
4
5
6

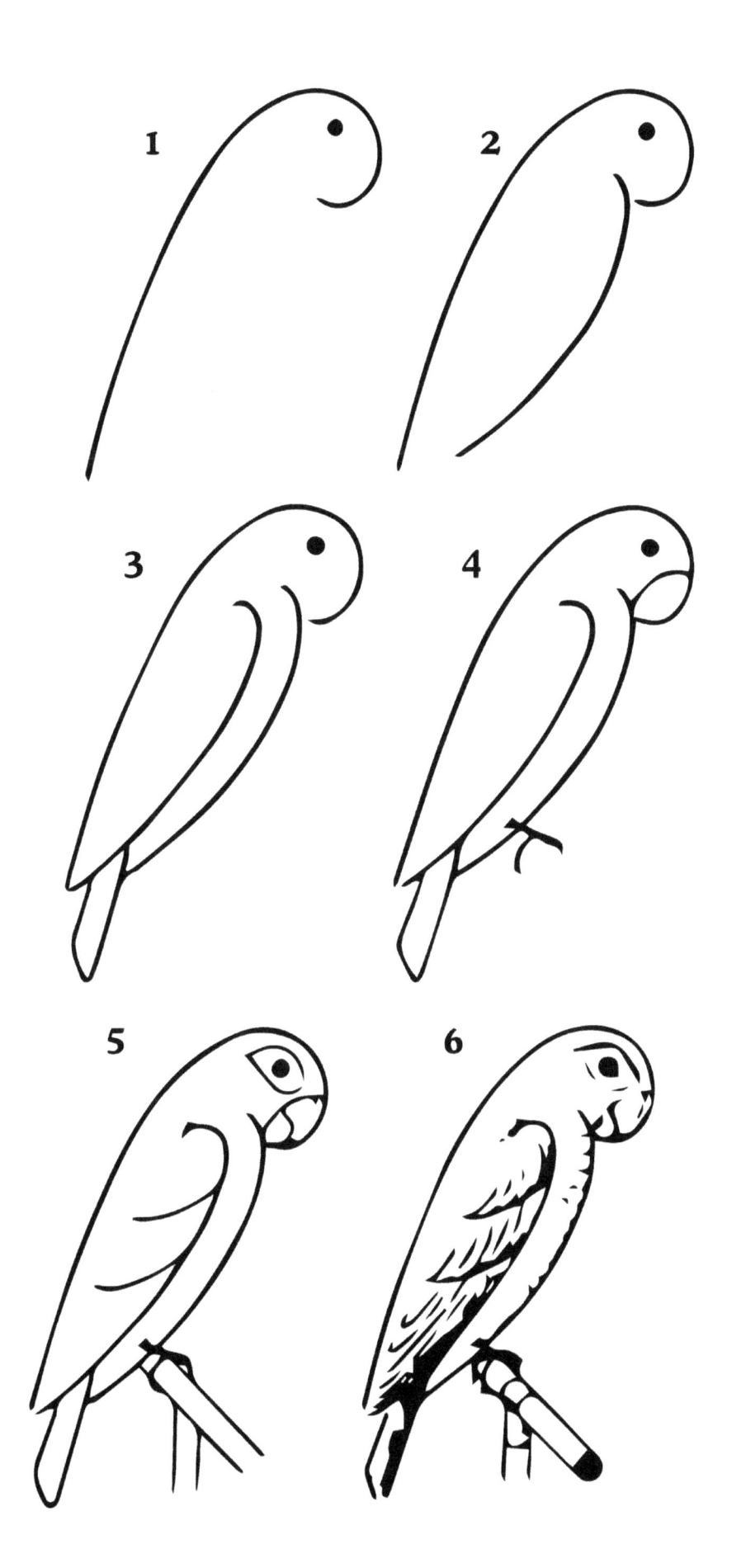

91

SWALLOWS

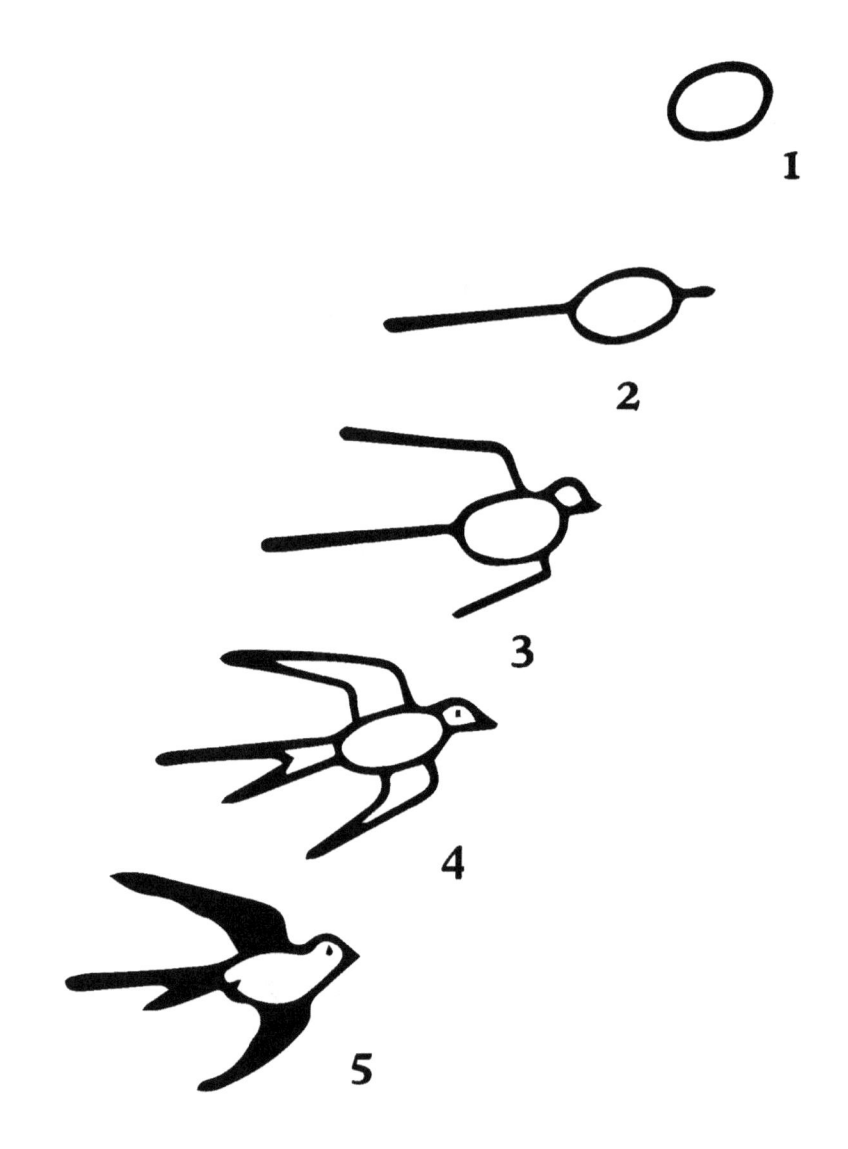

1

2

3

4

5

1

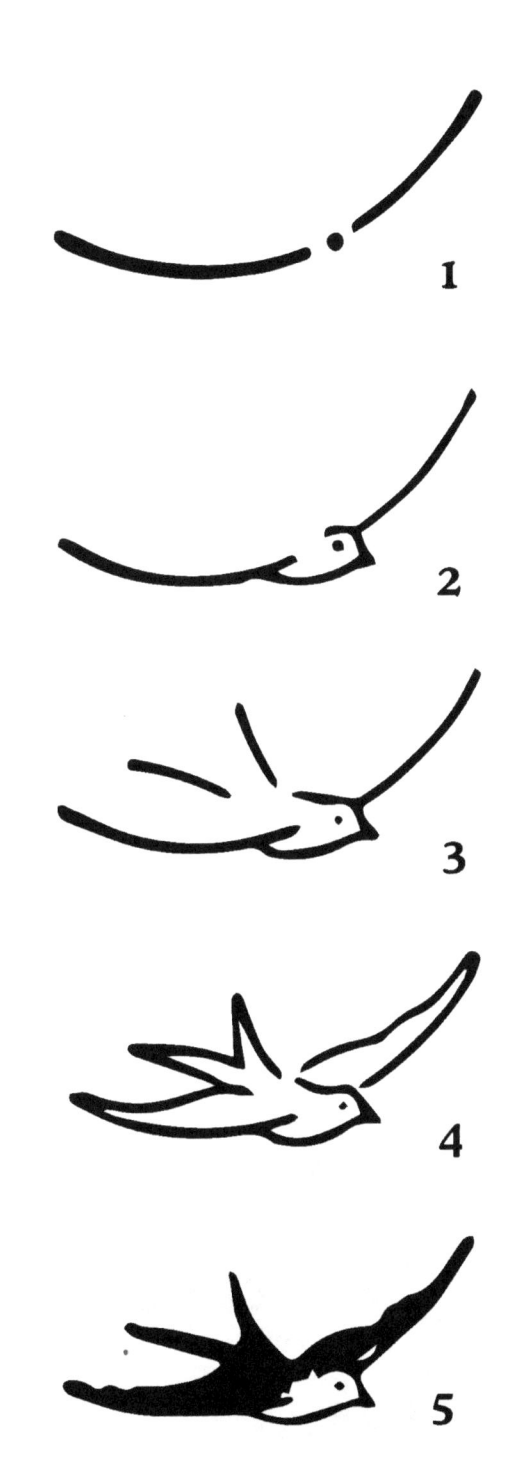

2

3

4

5

1

2

3

4

5

1

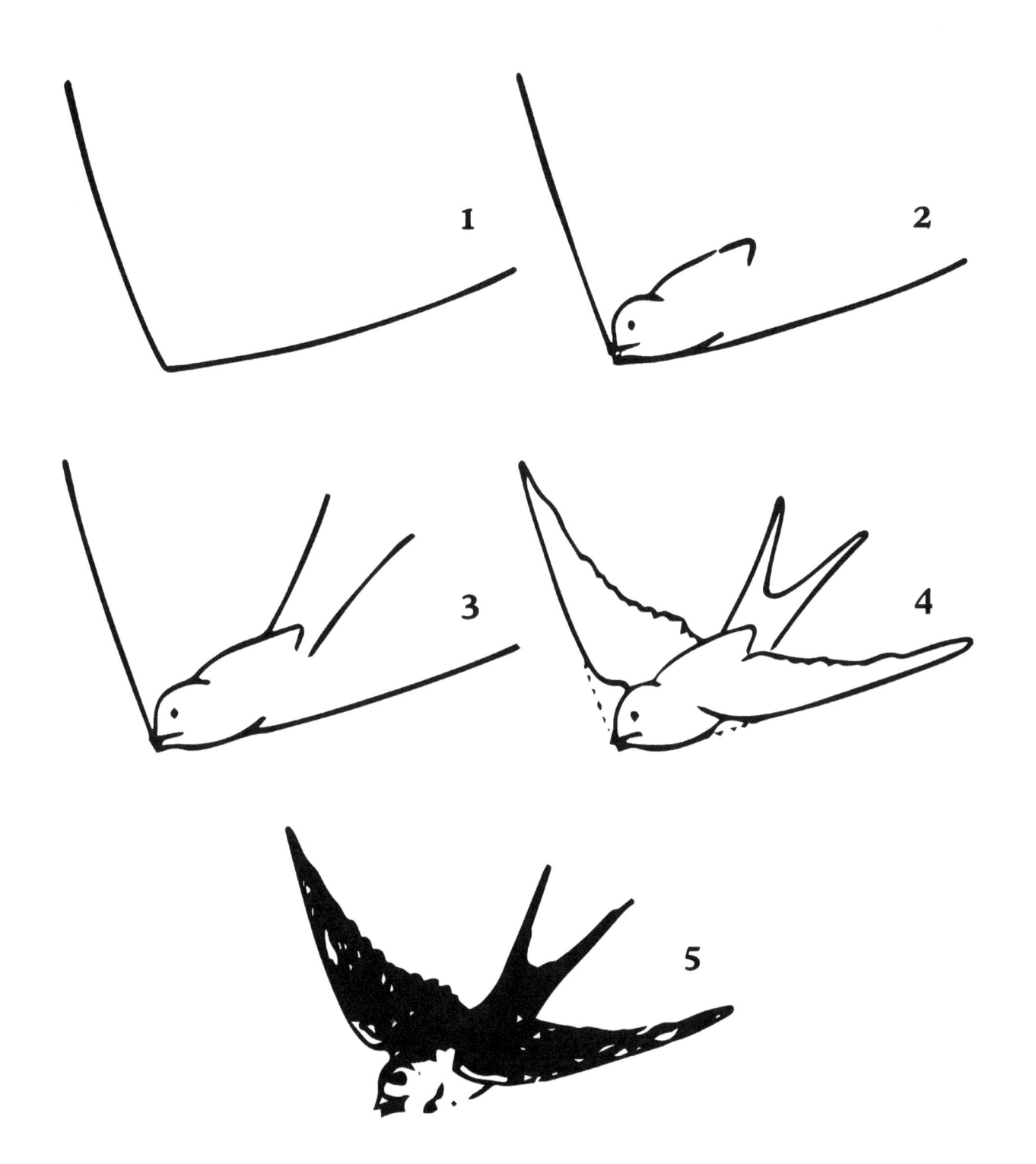

2

3

4

5

1
2
3
4
5

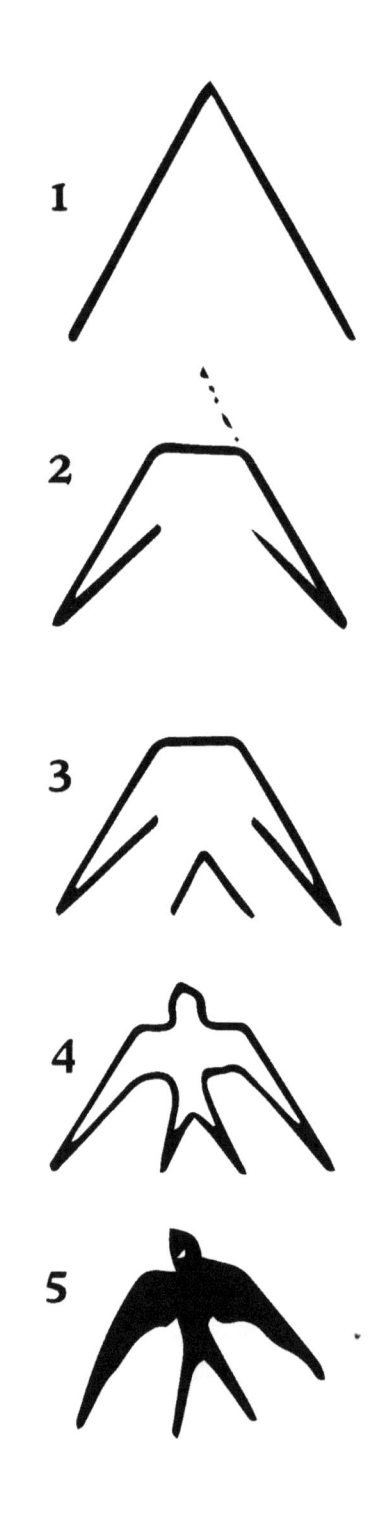

1

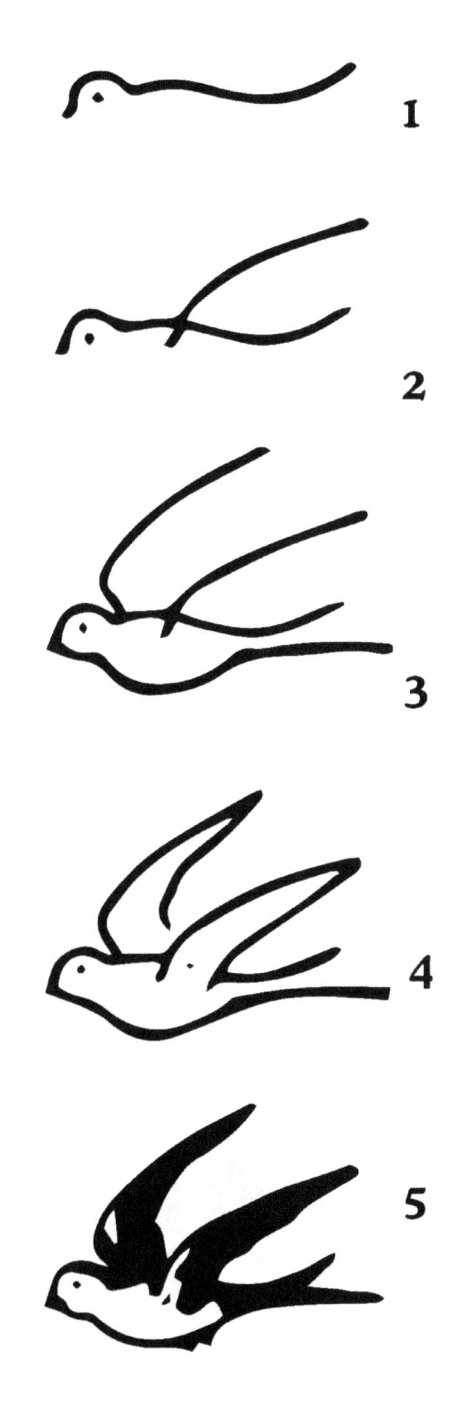

2

3

4

5

1

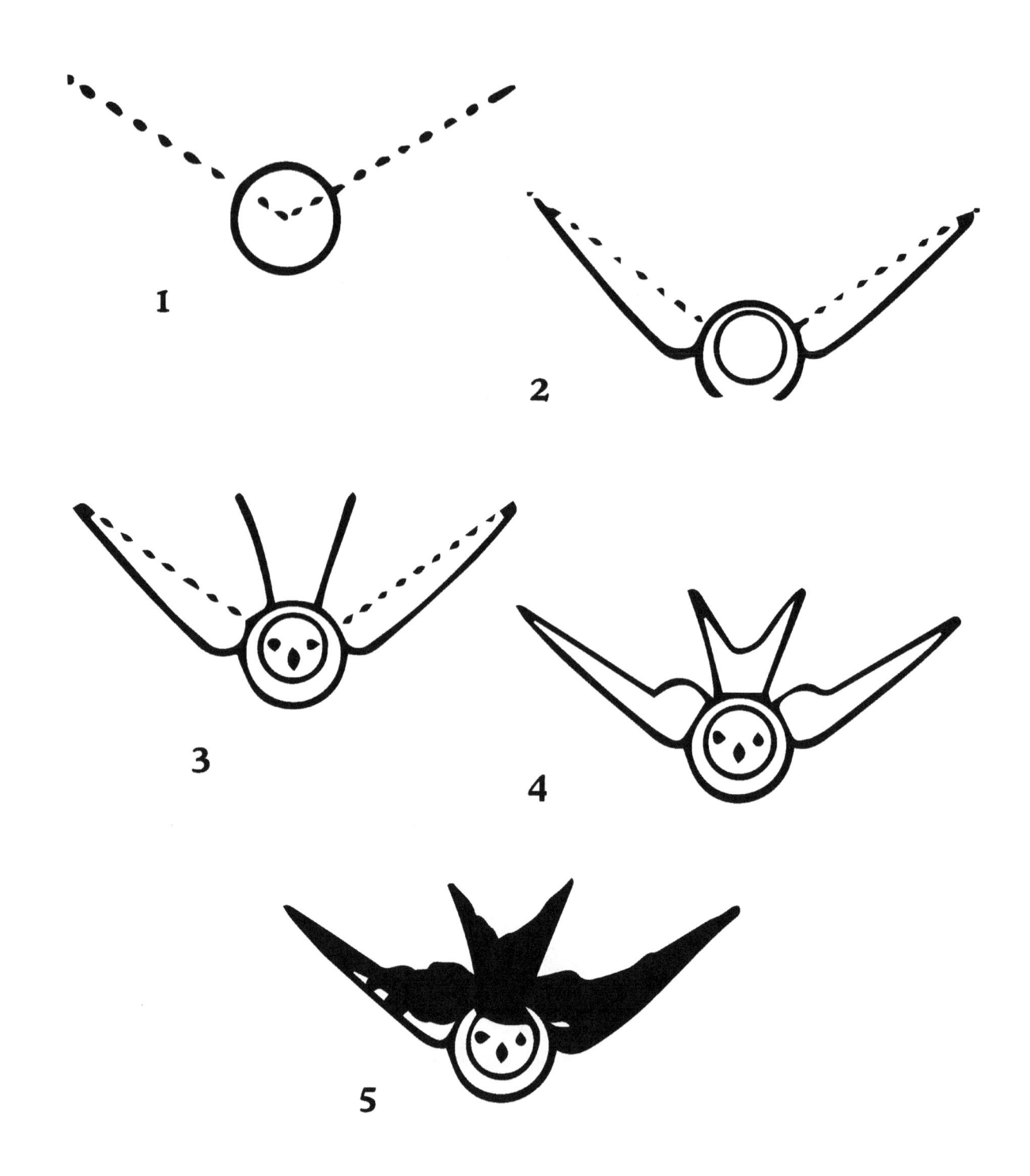

2

3

4

5

99

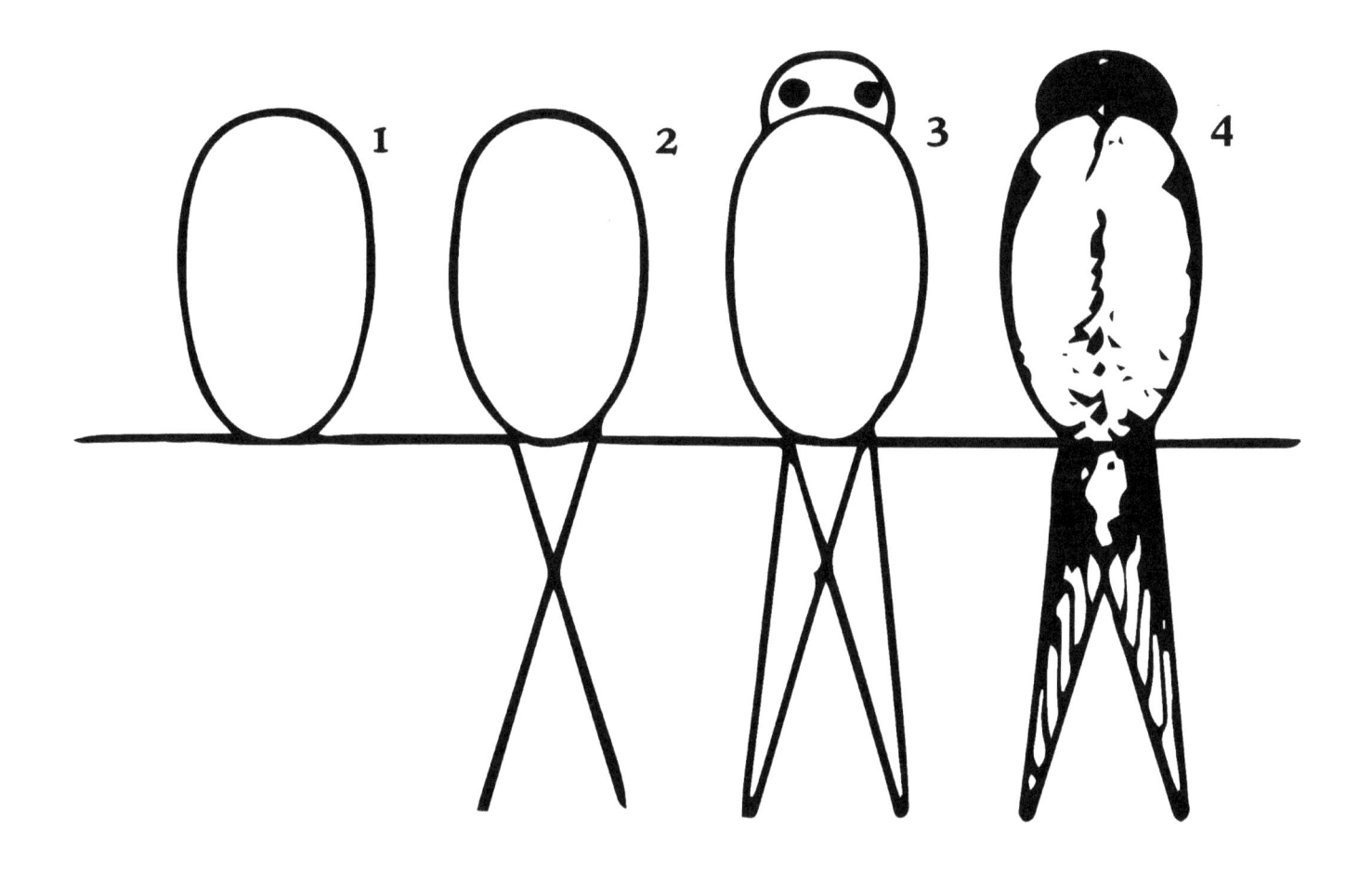

1 2 3 4

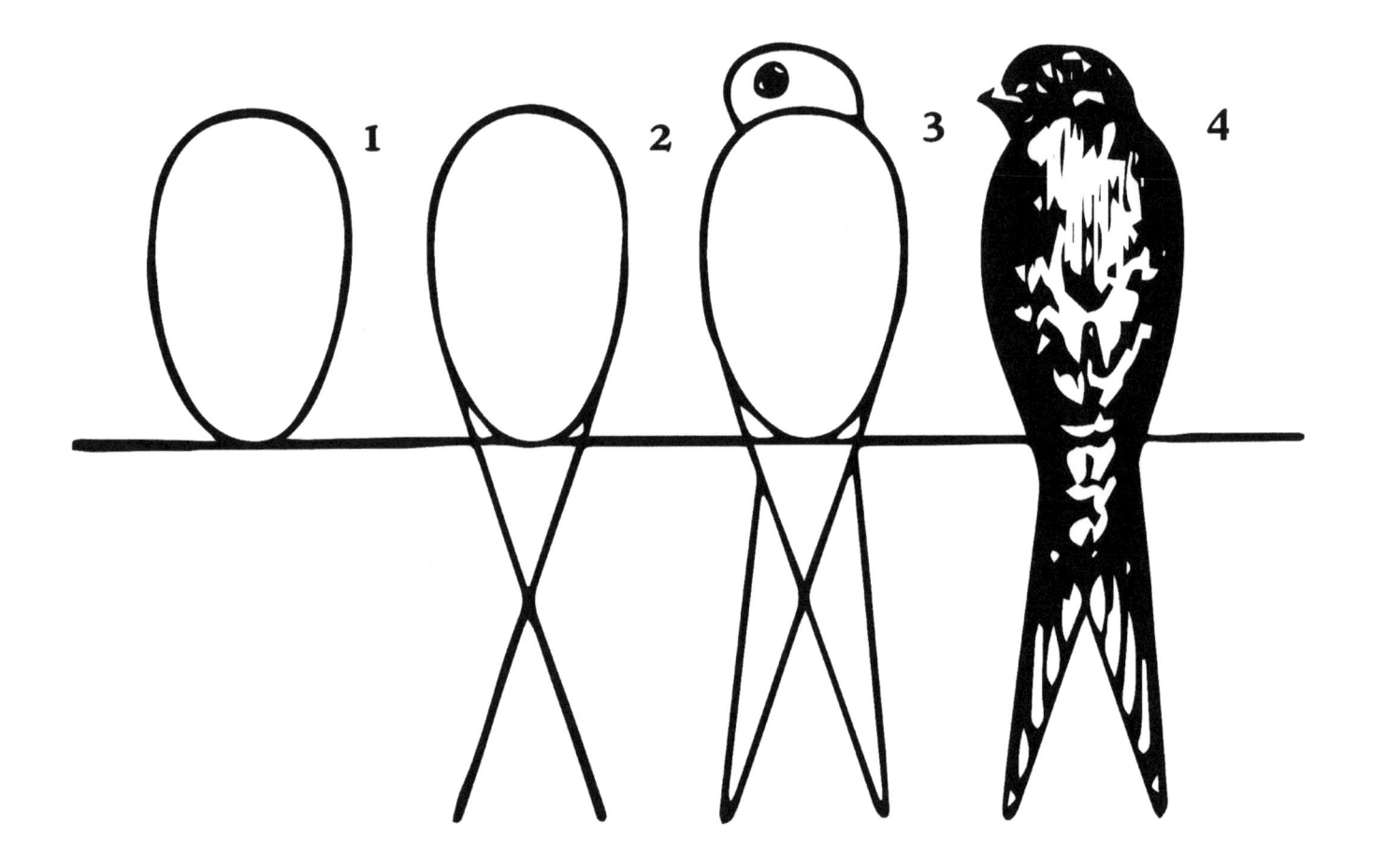

THRUSHES

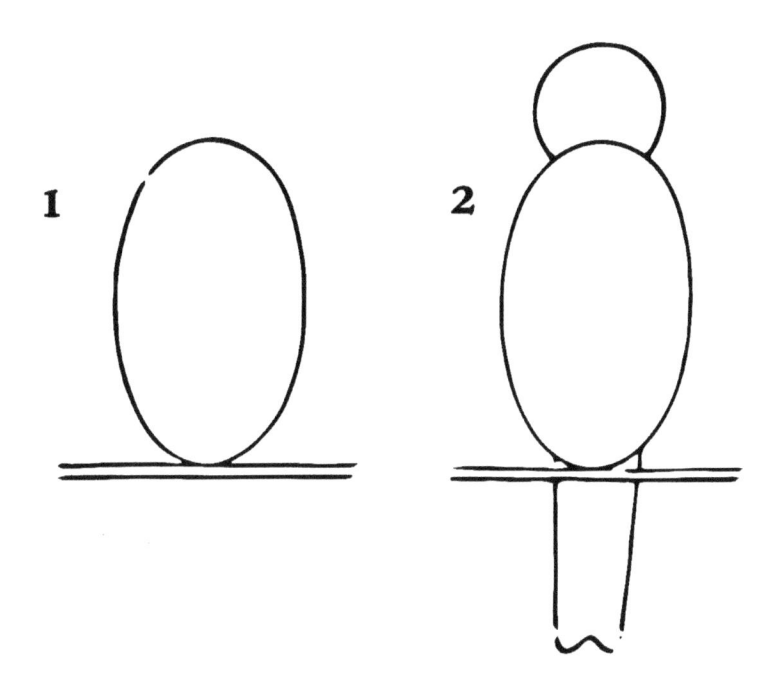

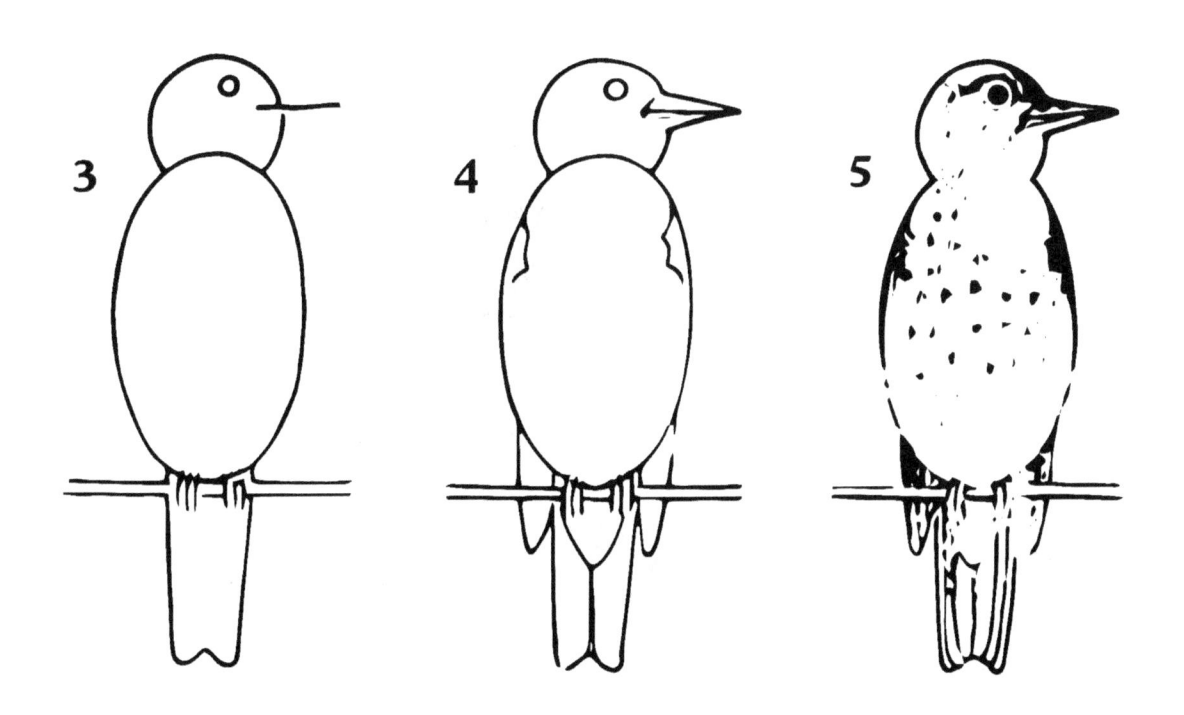

1
2
3
4
5

1

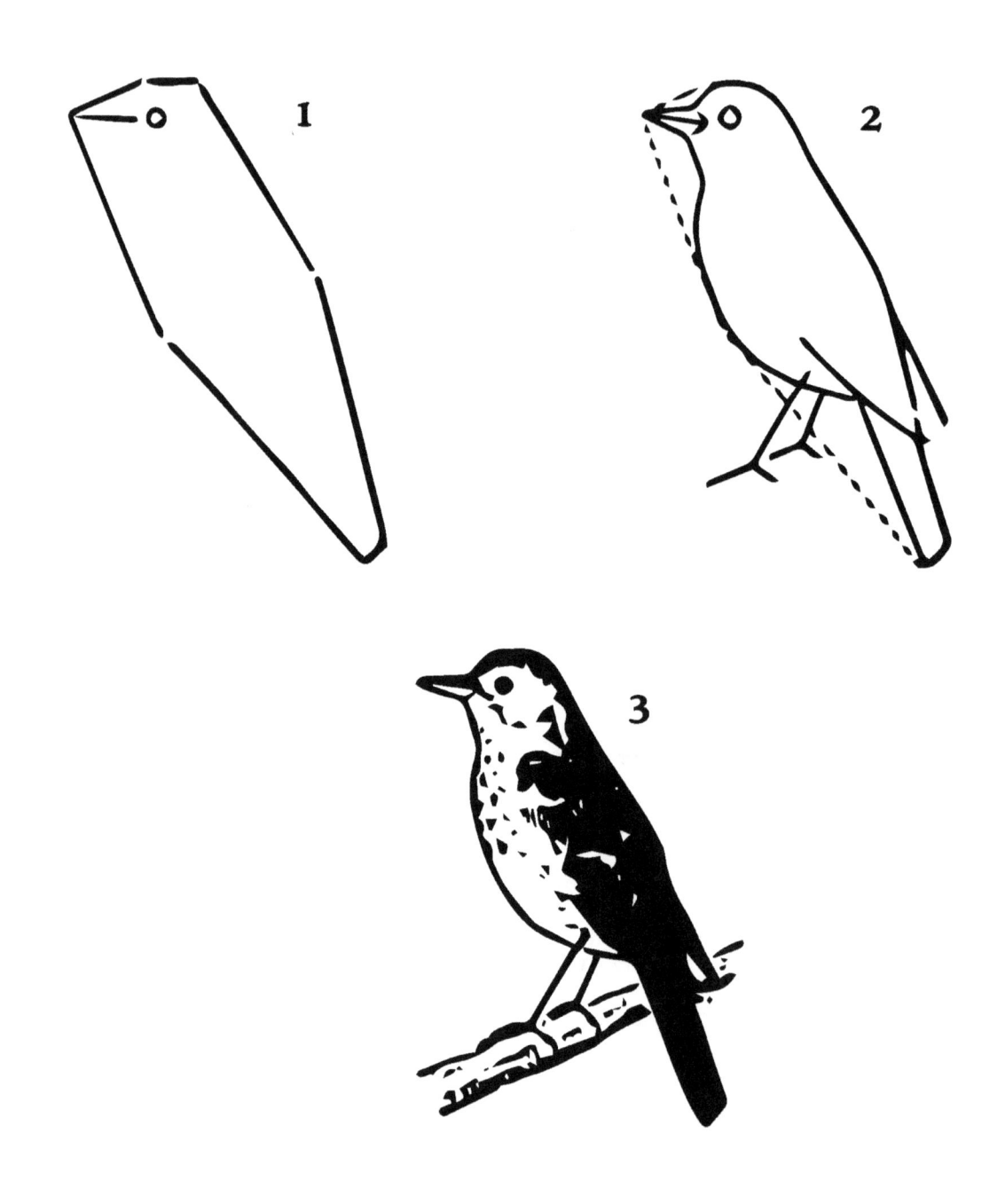

2

3

PENGUIN

STORK

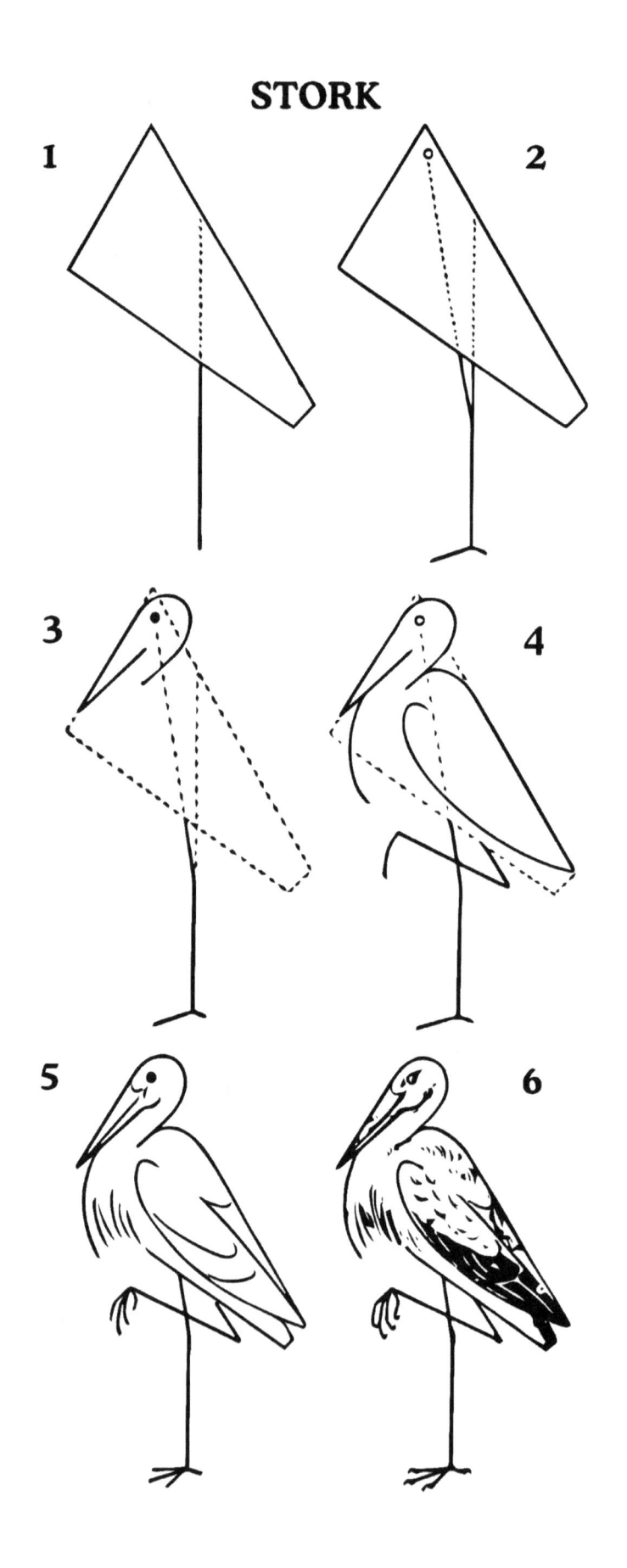

HERONS

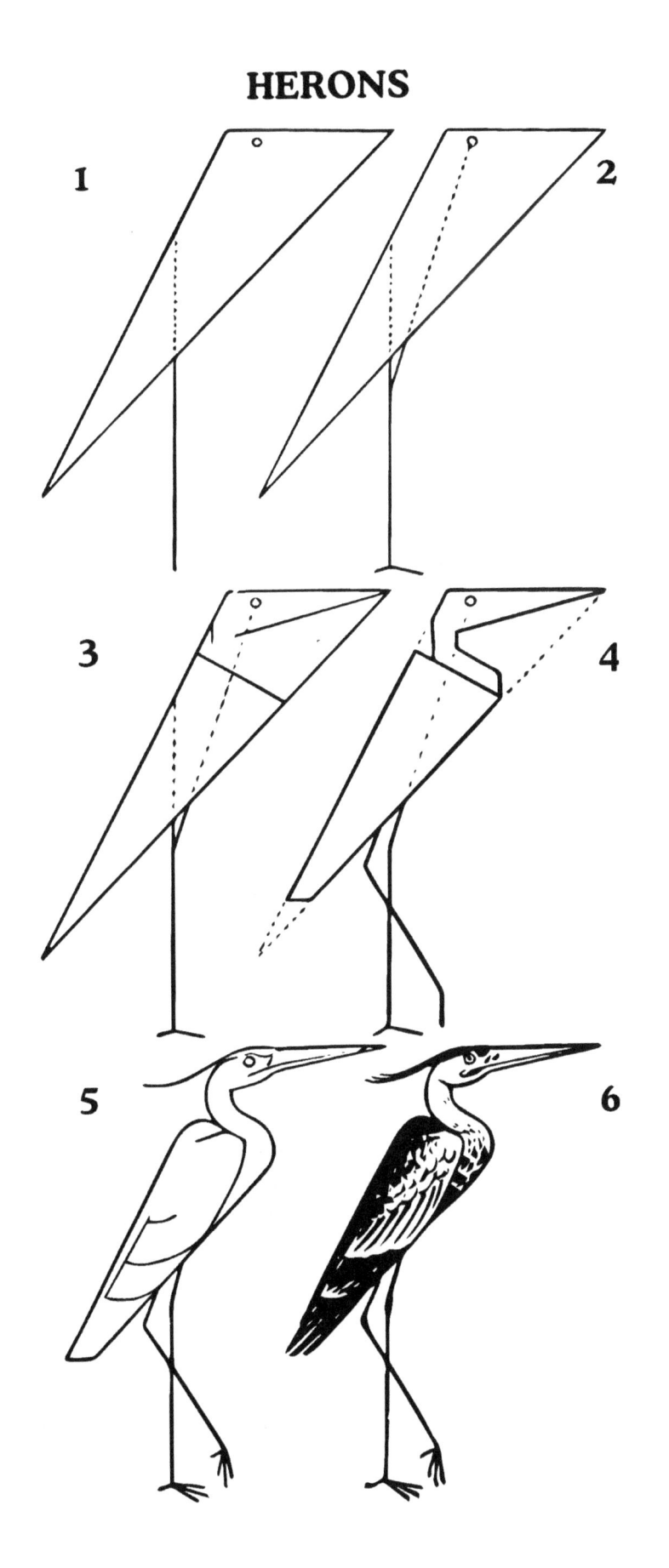

105

1 2

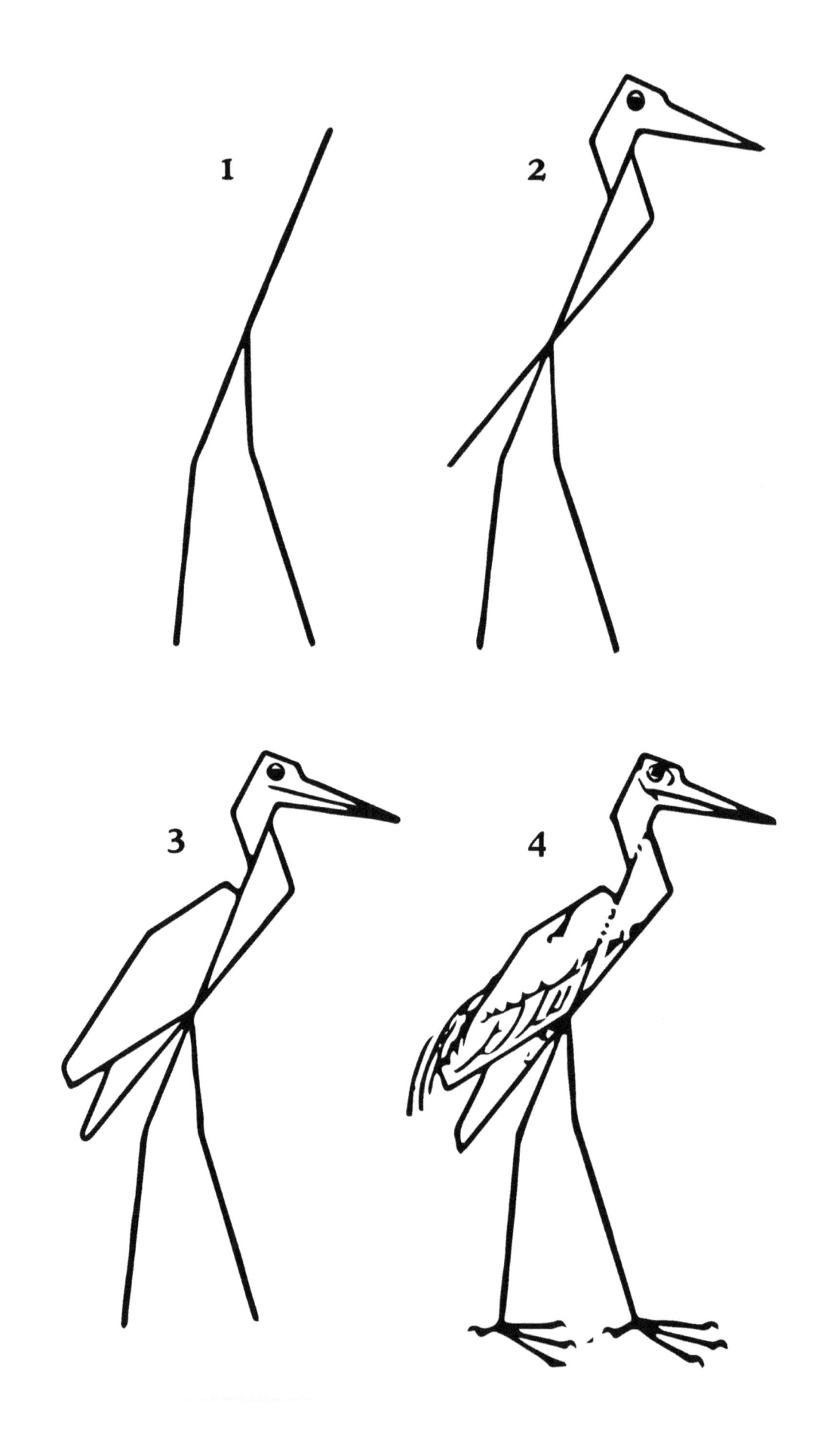

3 4

FLICKER

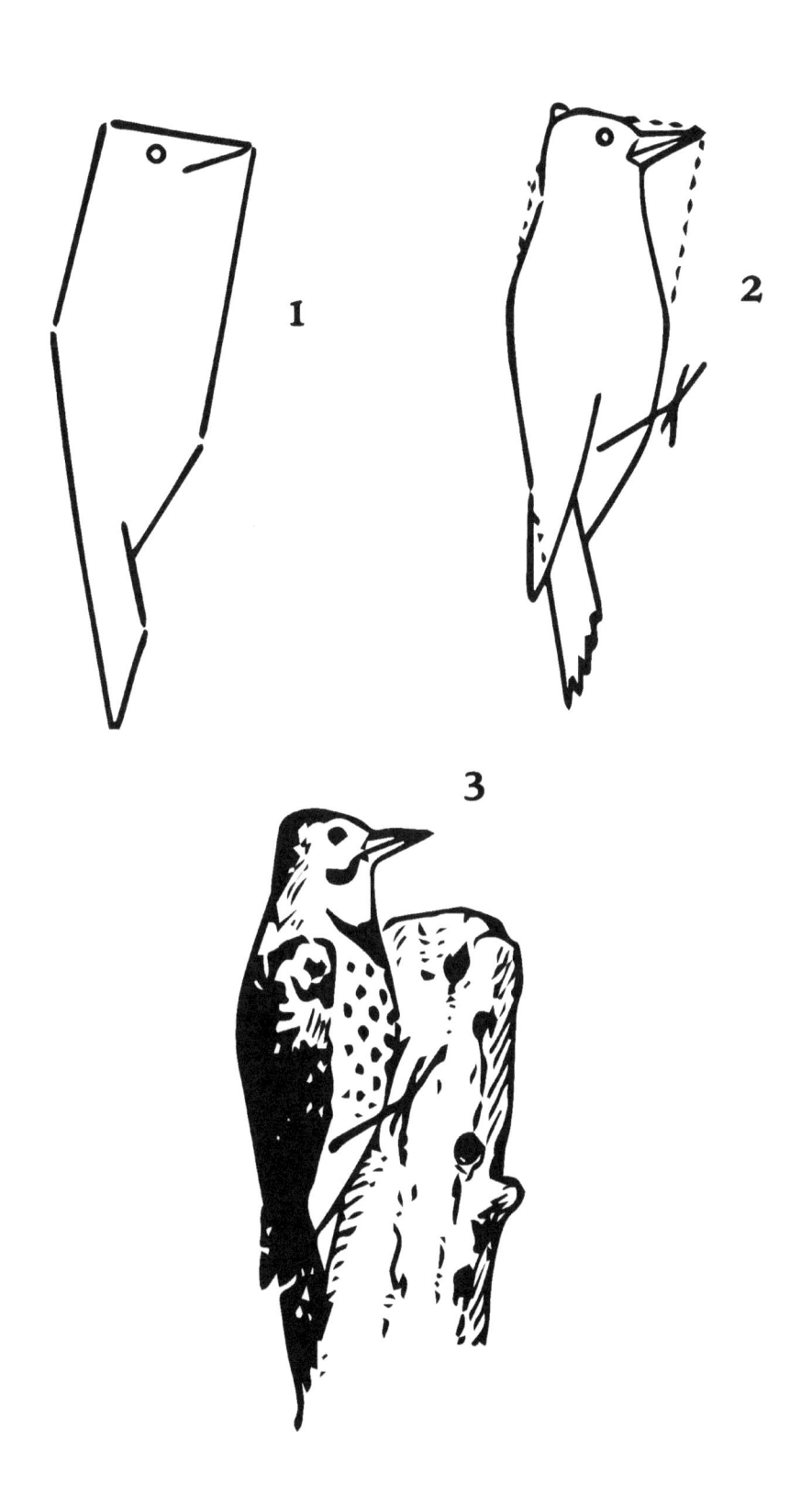

1

2

3

SEAGULL

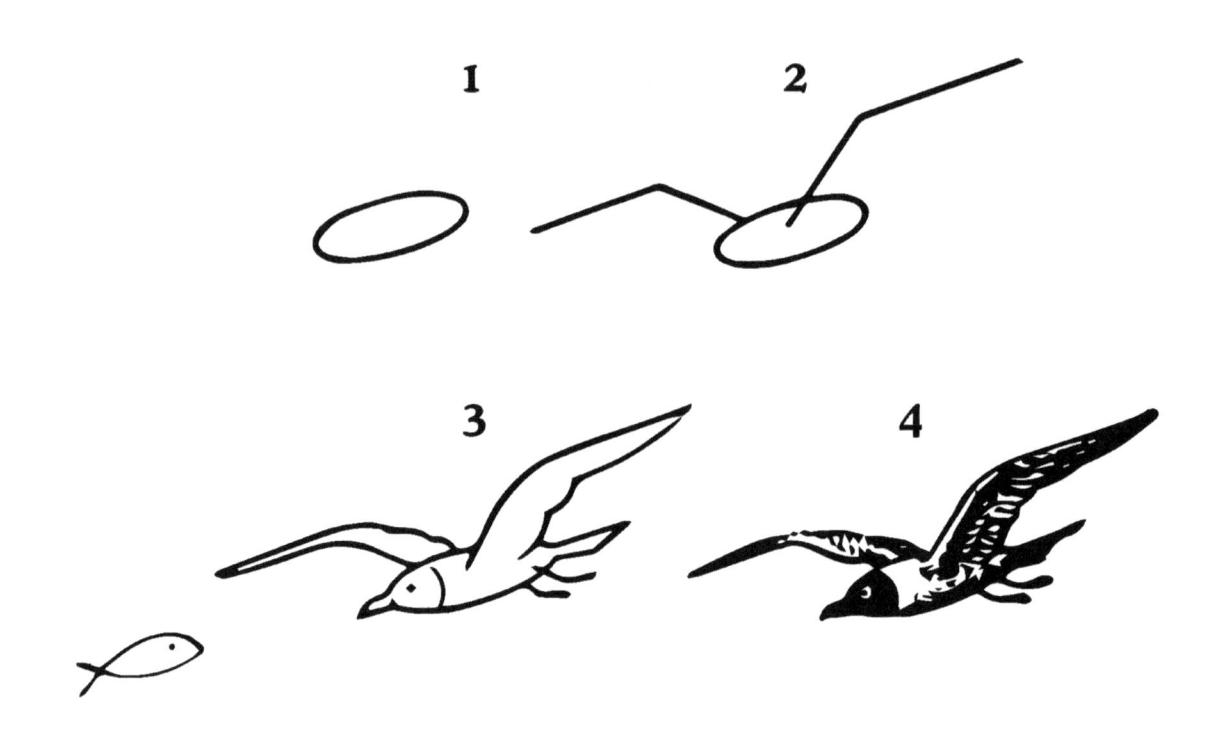

CRANE

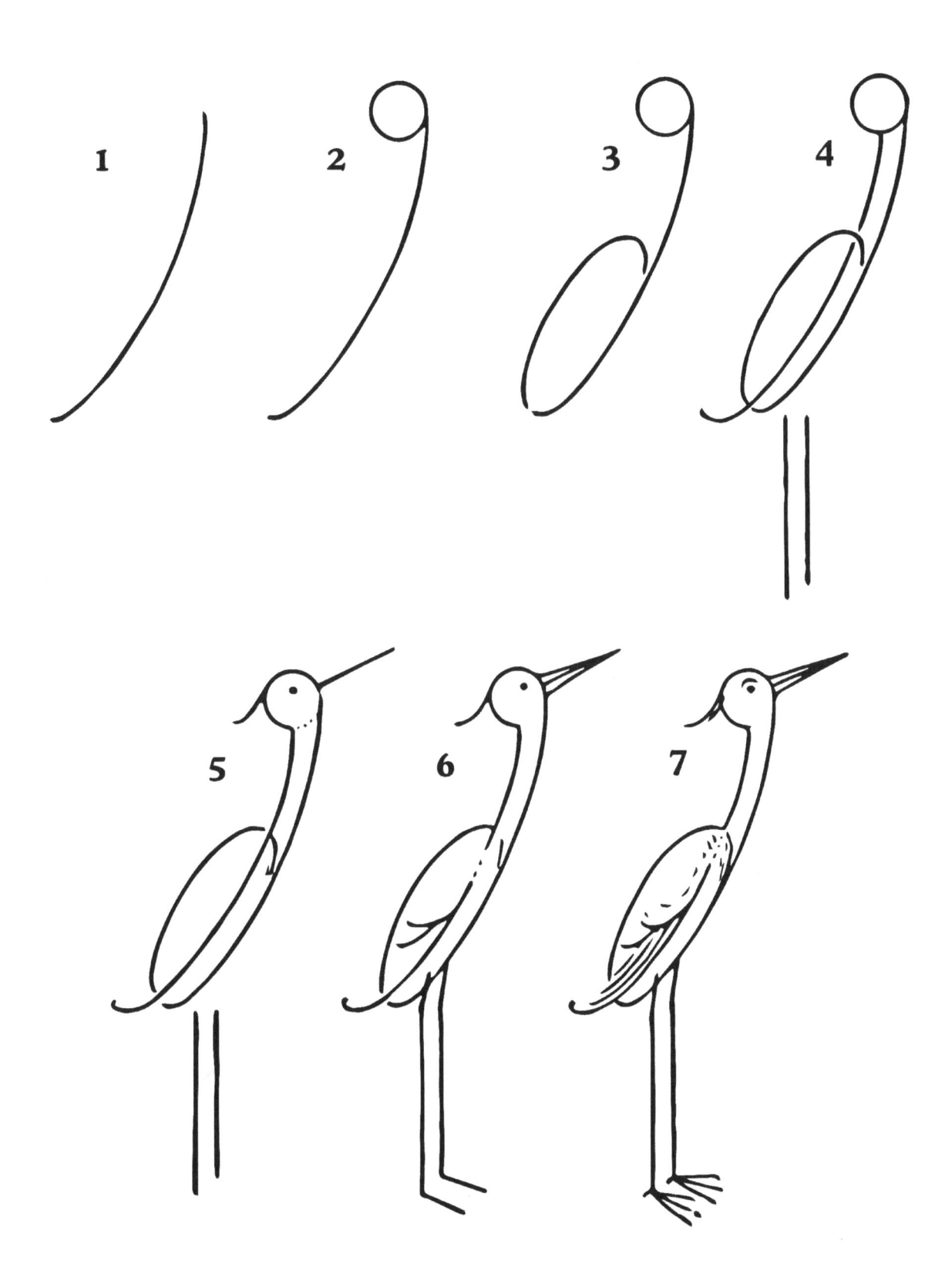

CRANE'S HEAD

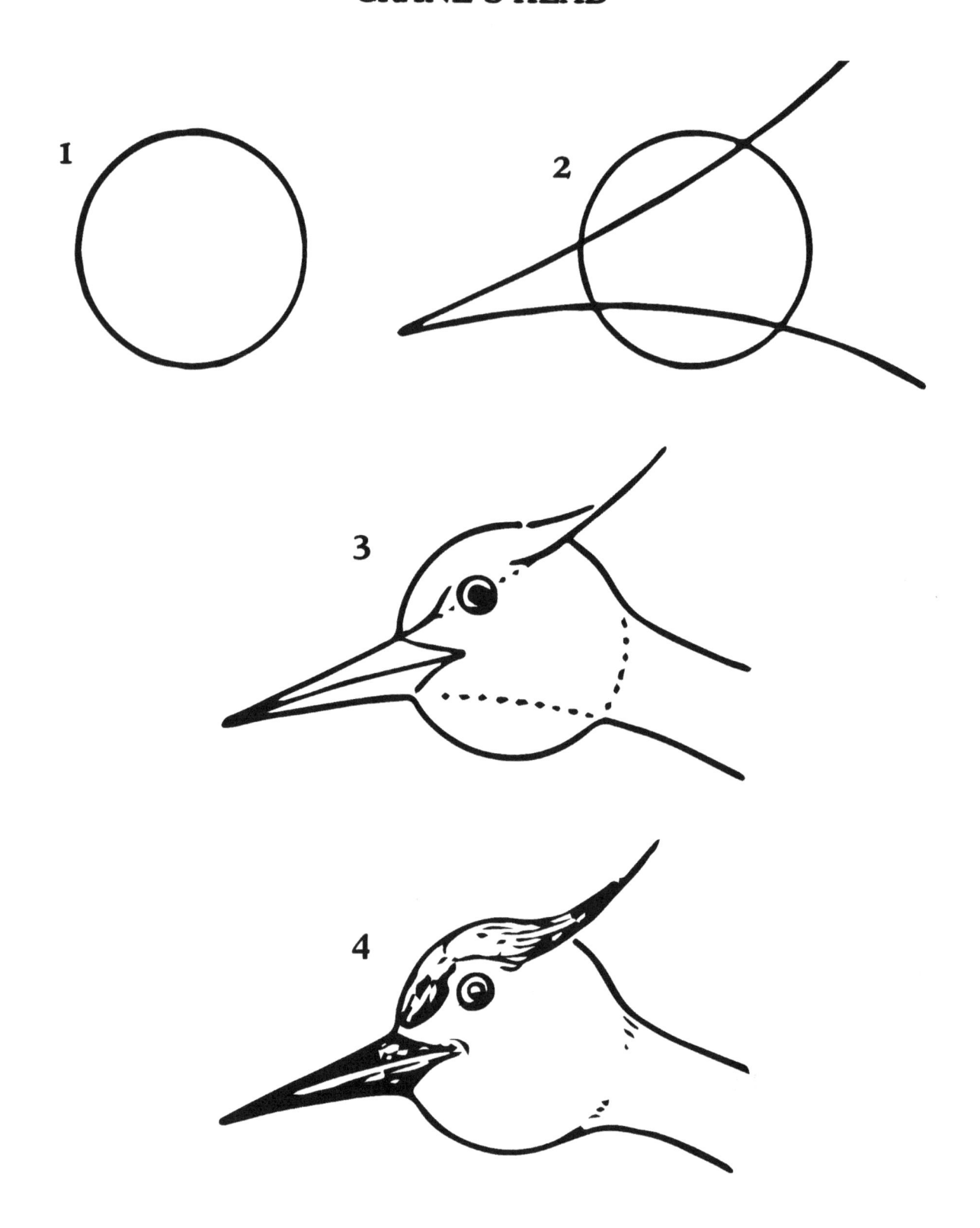

111

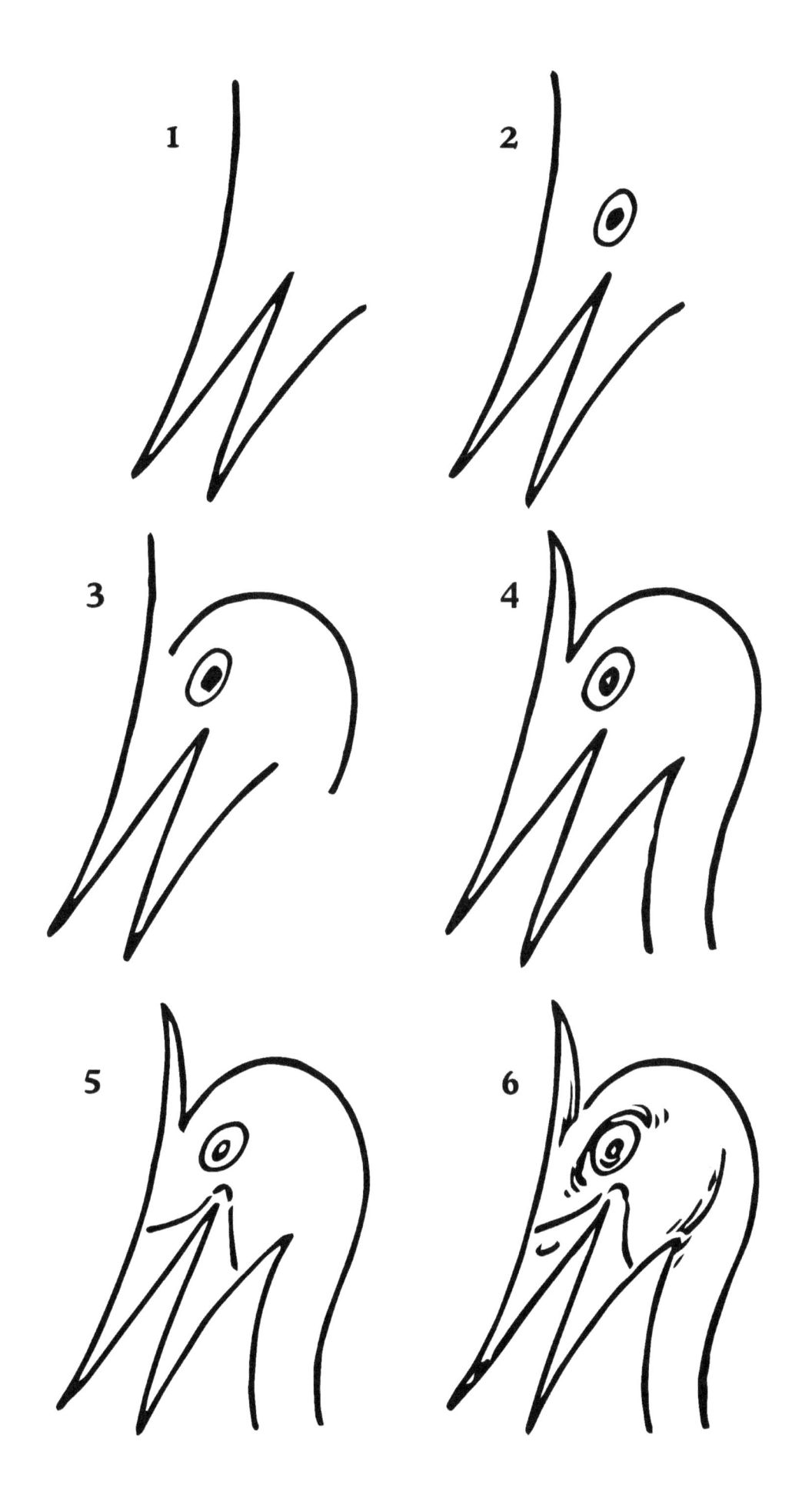

CRESTED CRANE

SWAN

TURKEY

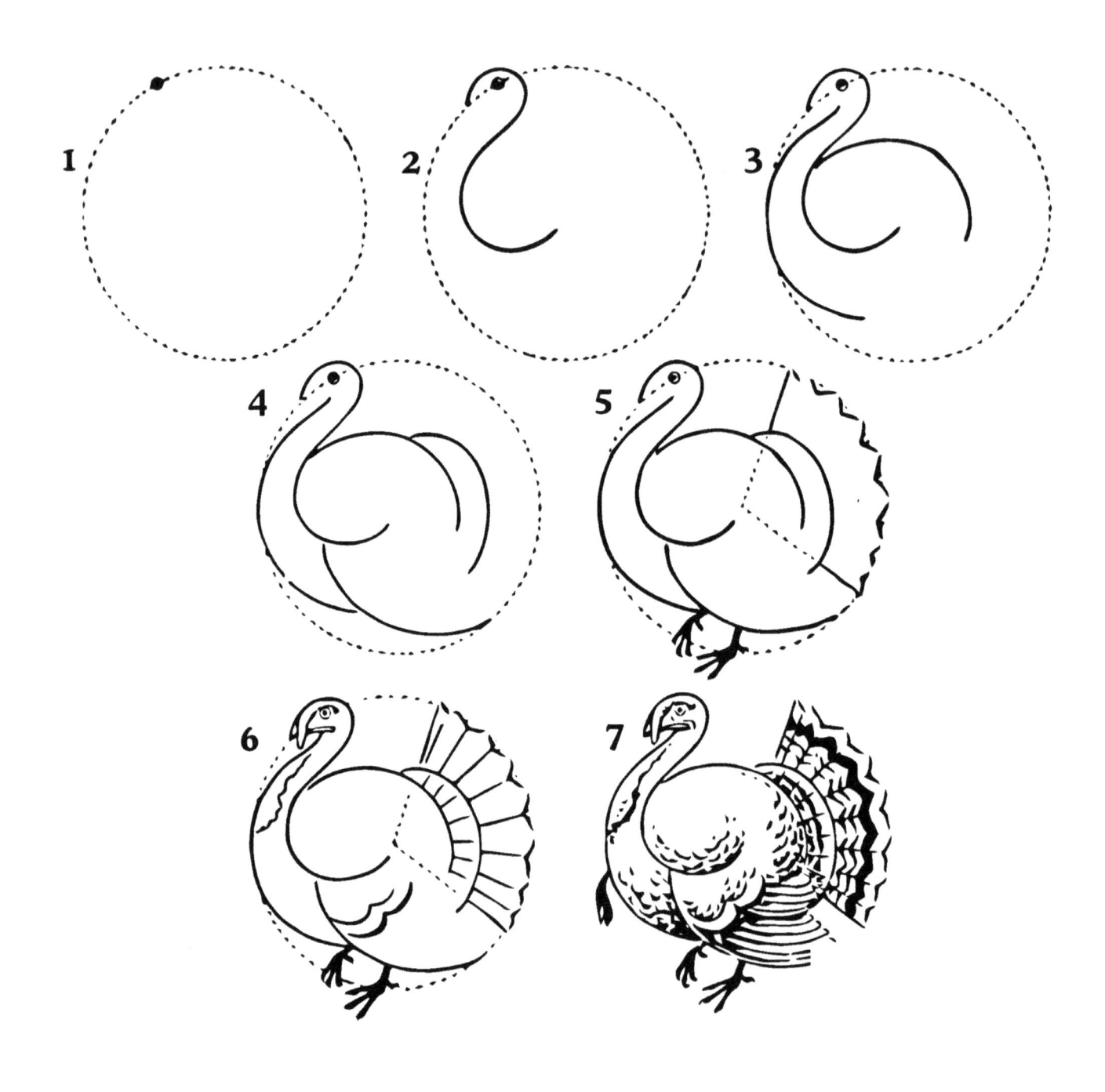

FANTAIL PIGEON

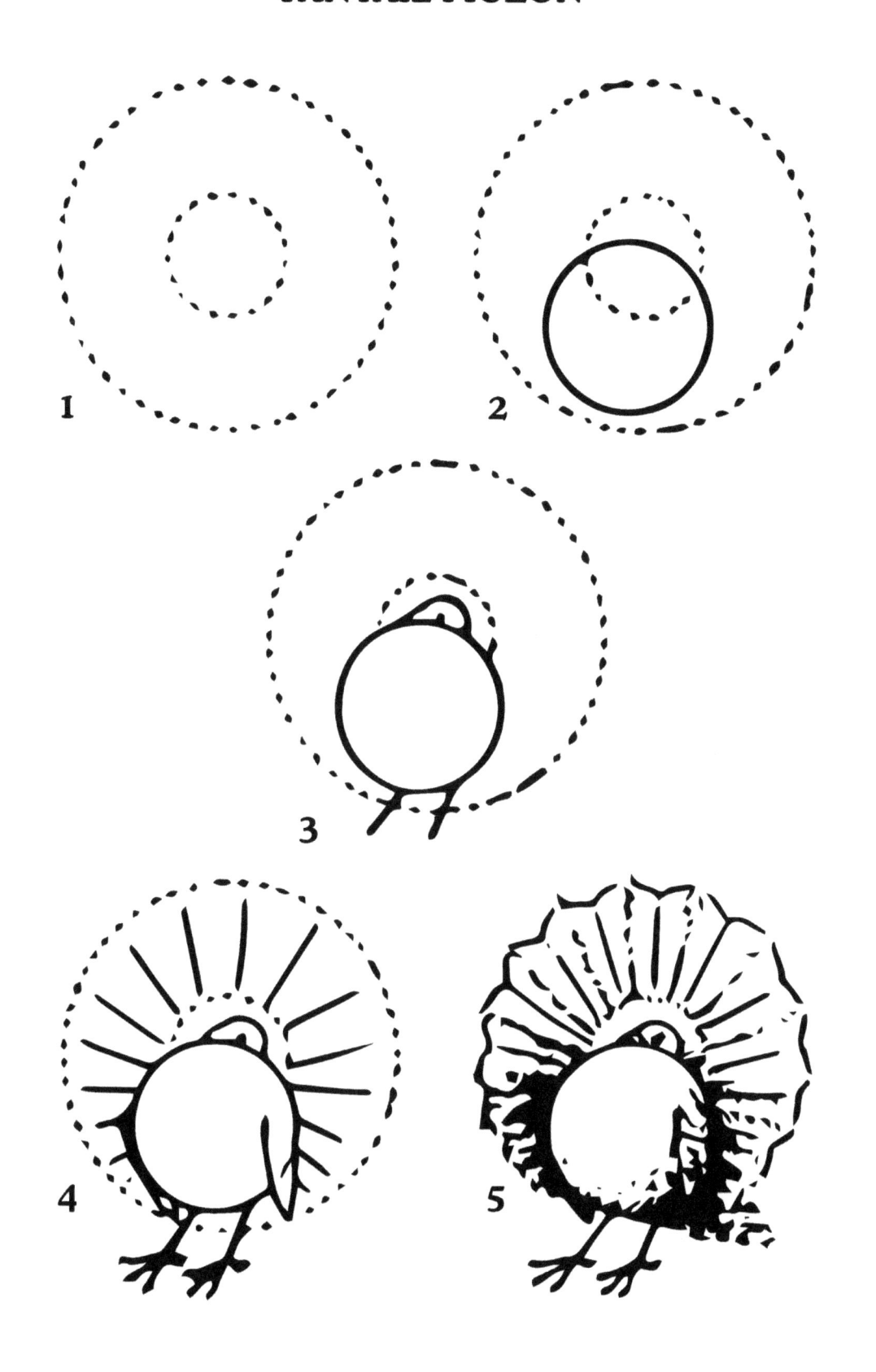

HUMMING BIRDS

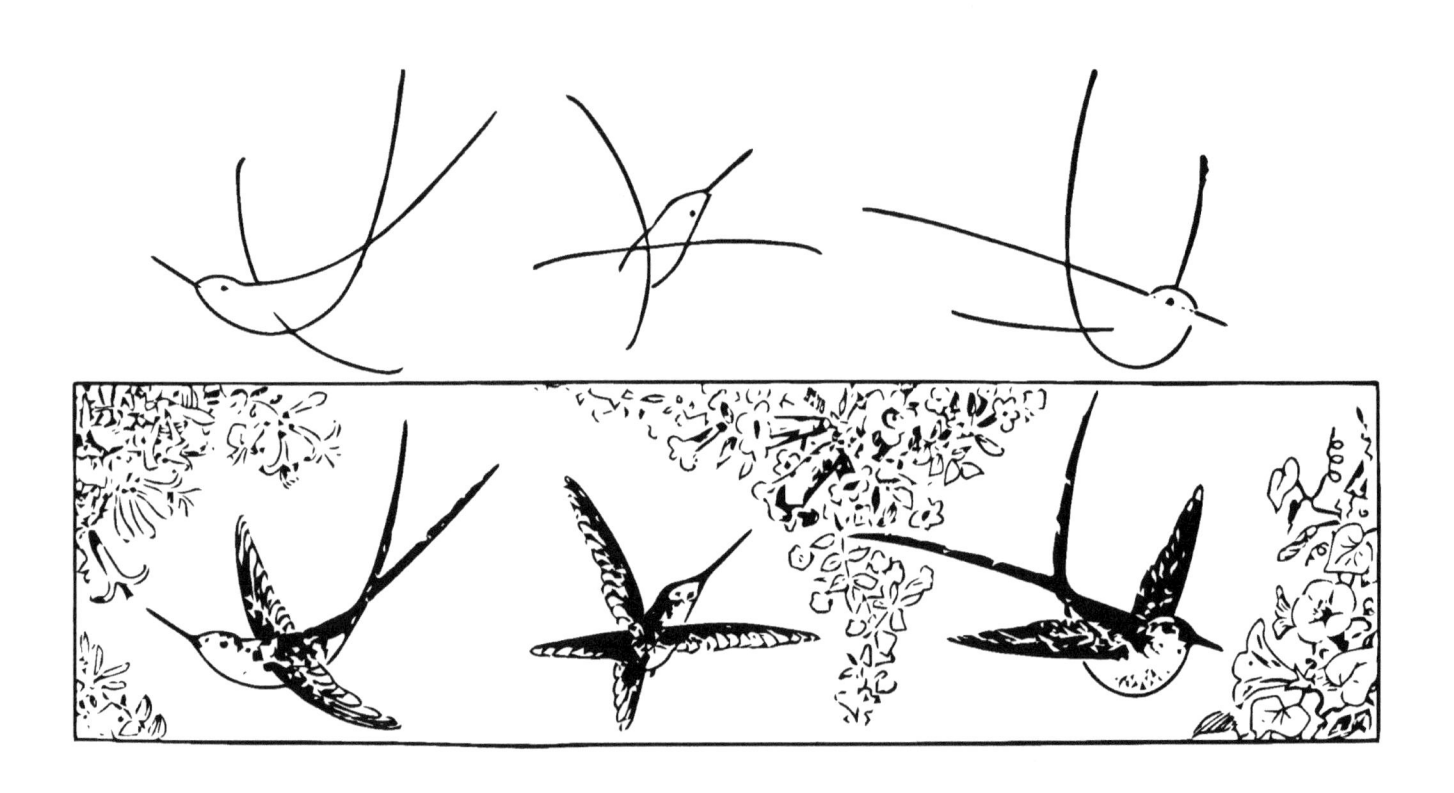

MAGPIE

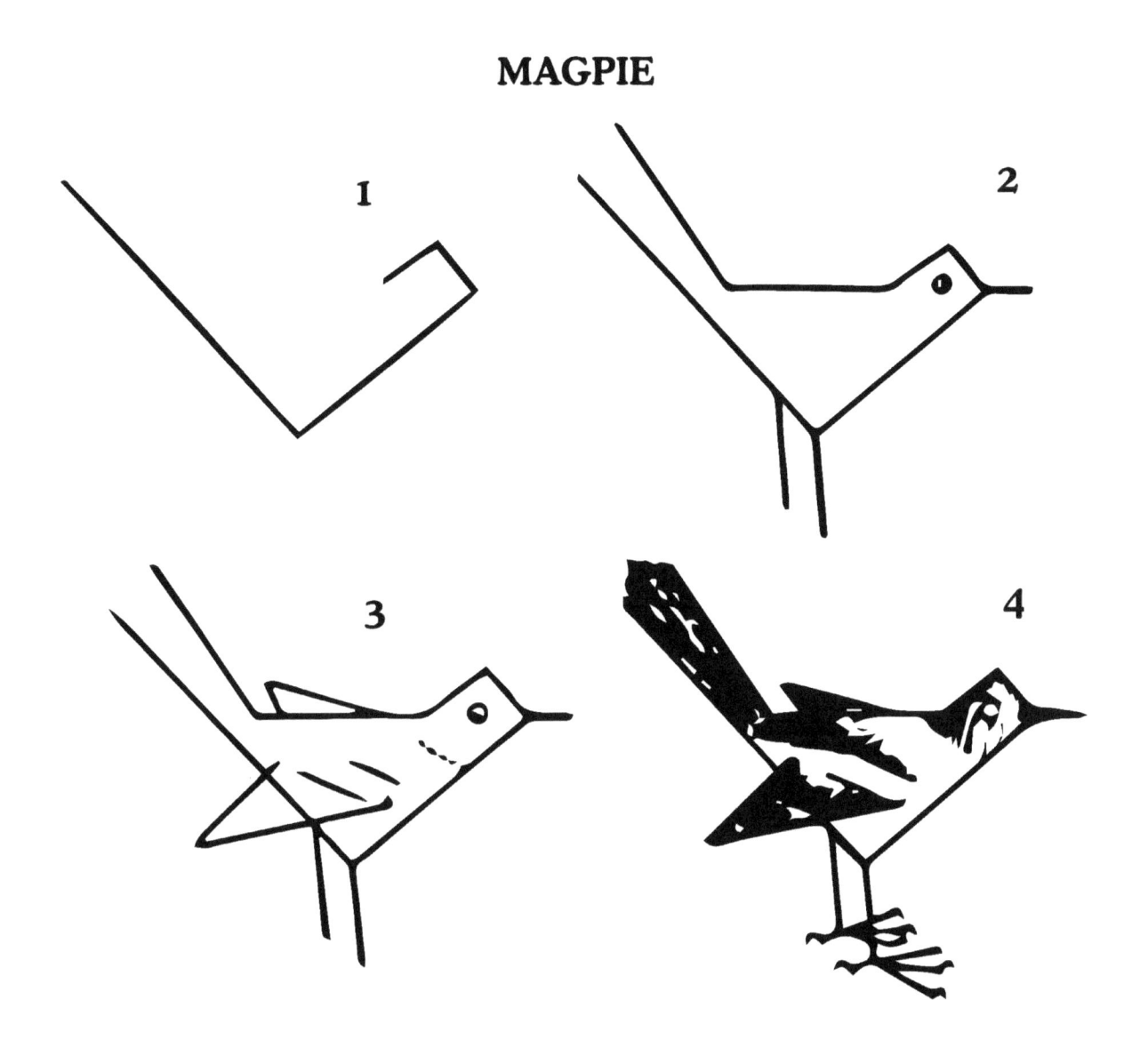

1
2
3
4

ADJUTANT

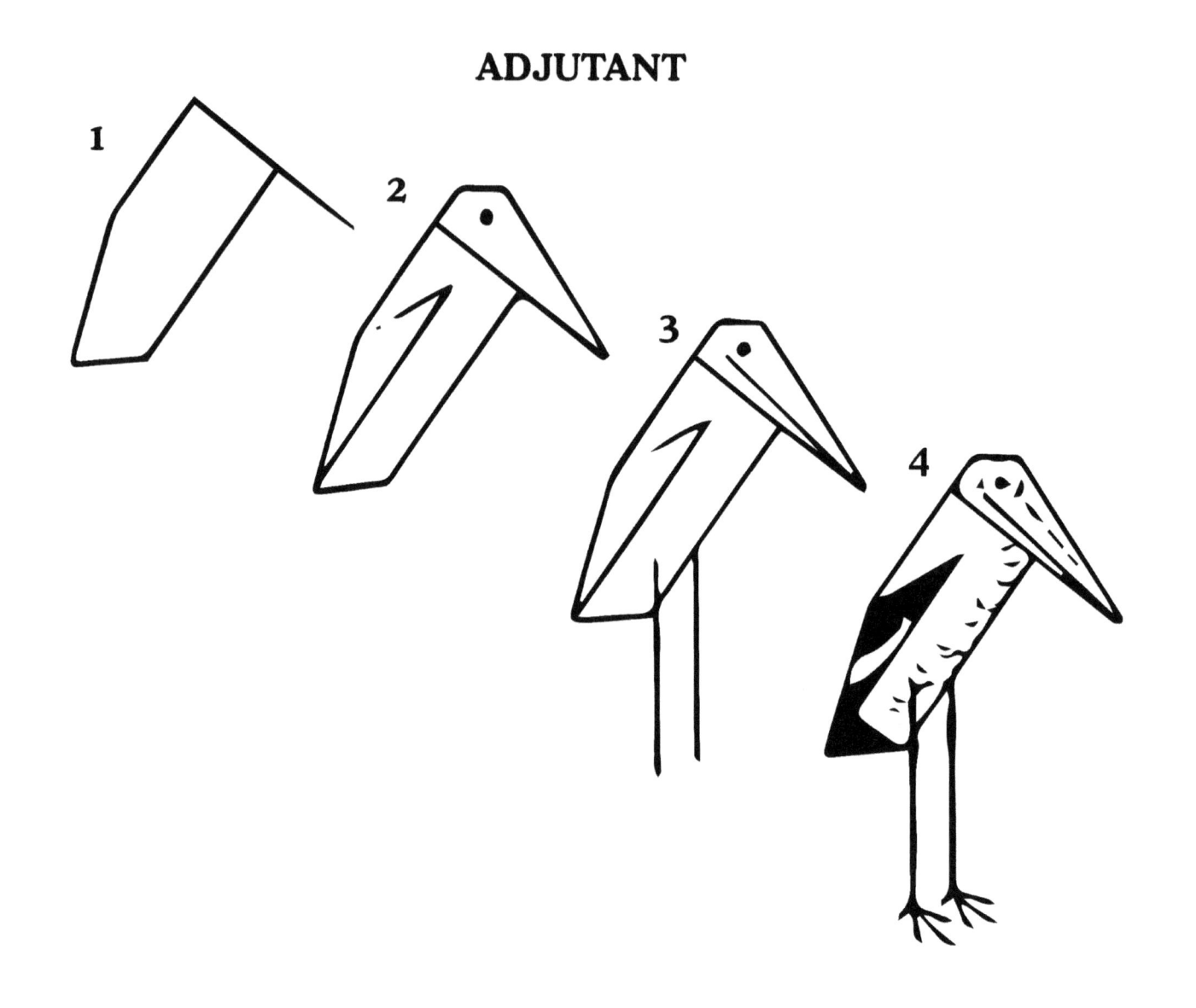

STILT

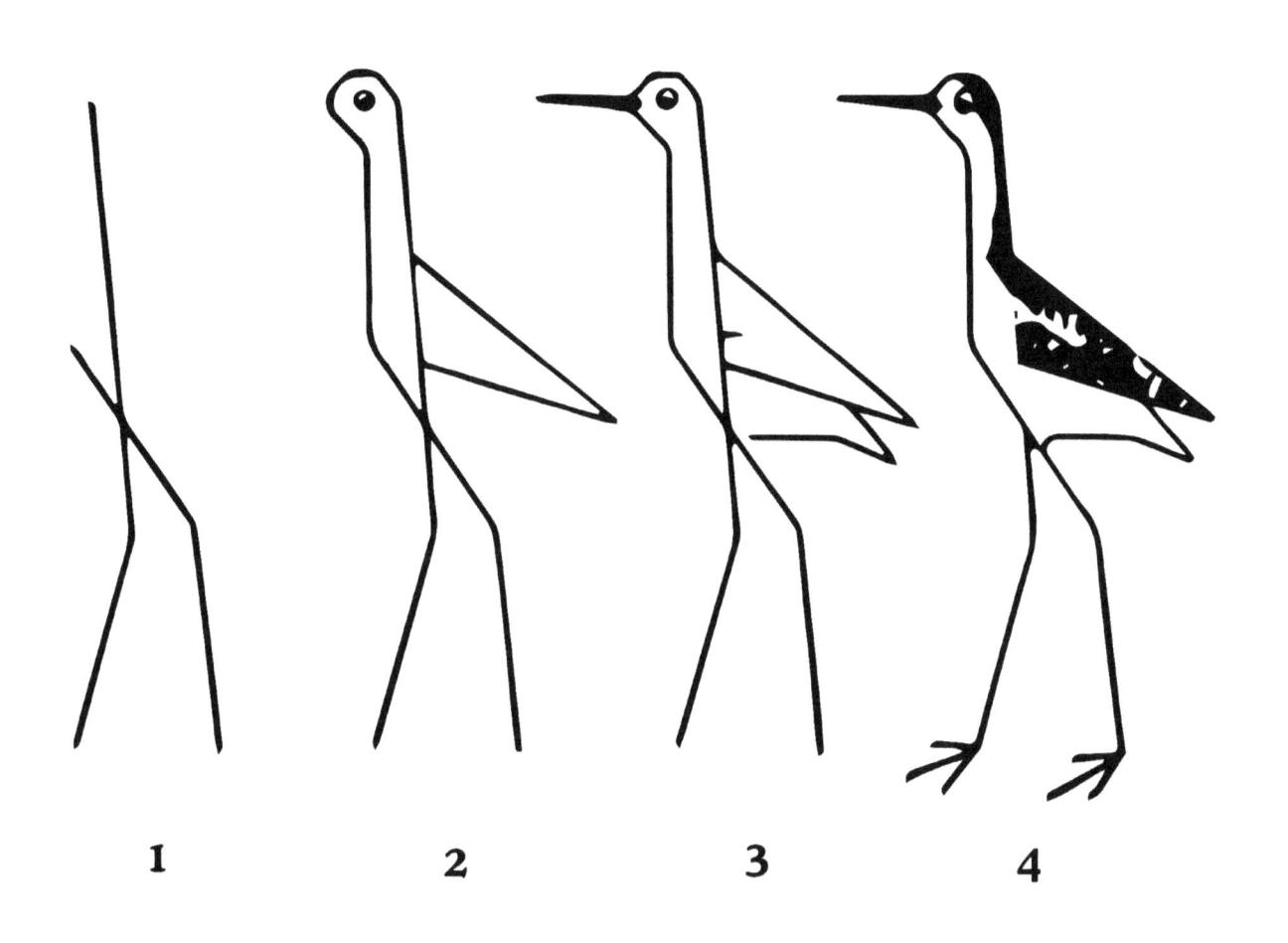

1   2   3   4

PELICAN

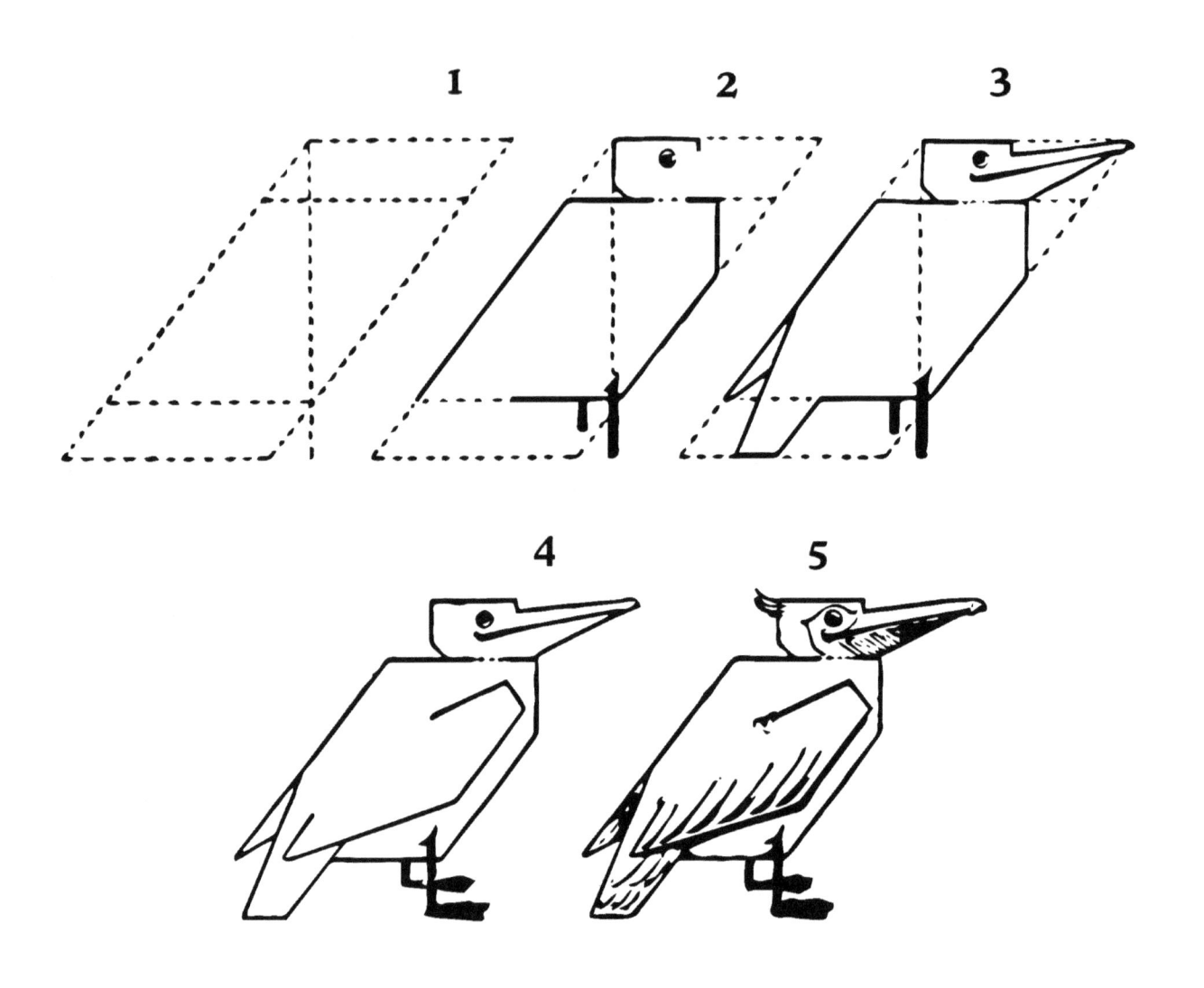

1 2 3

4 5

VARIOUS BIRDS

1
2
3
4
5
6

1

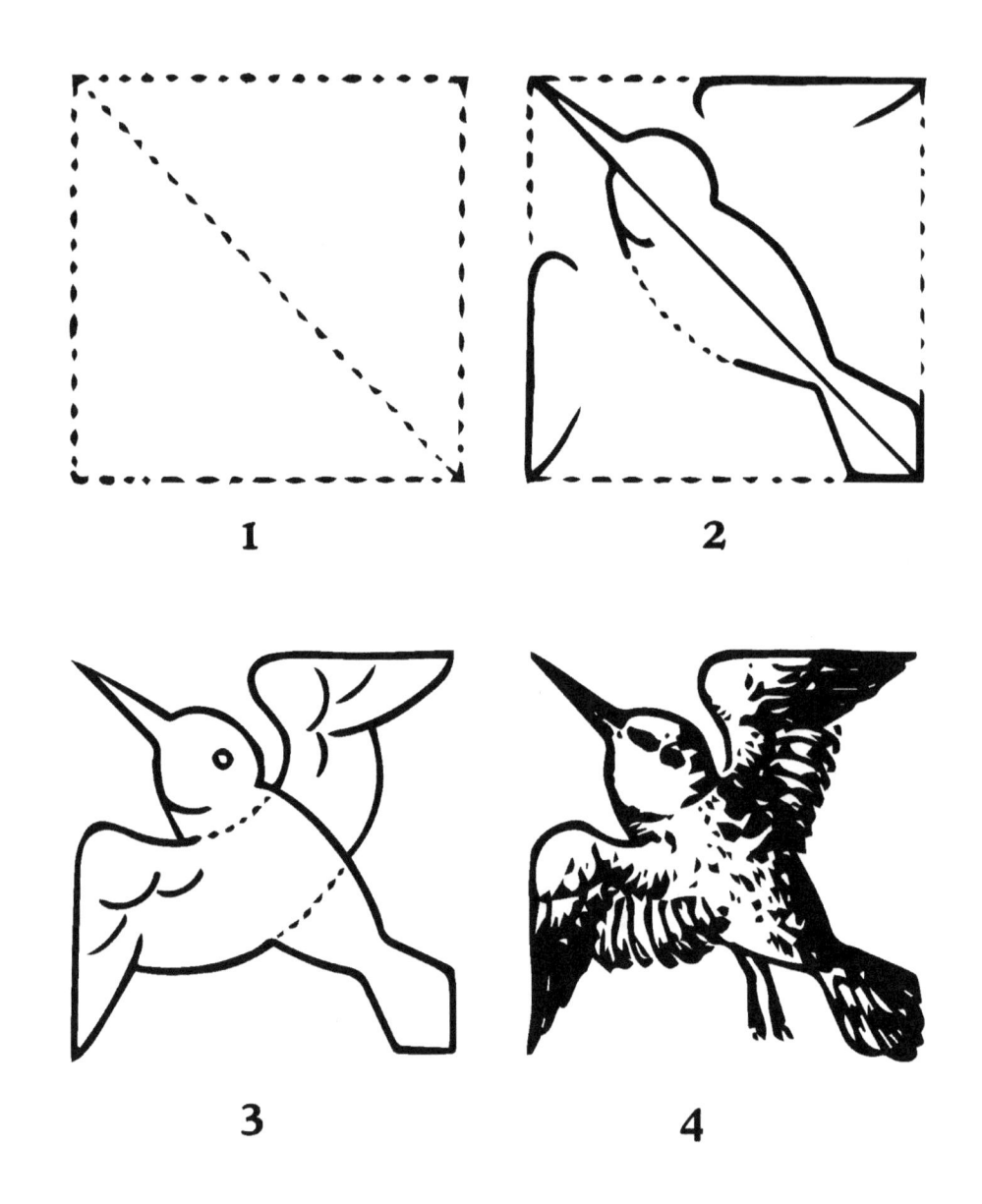

2

3

4

1 2

3 4

5 6

123

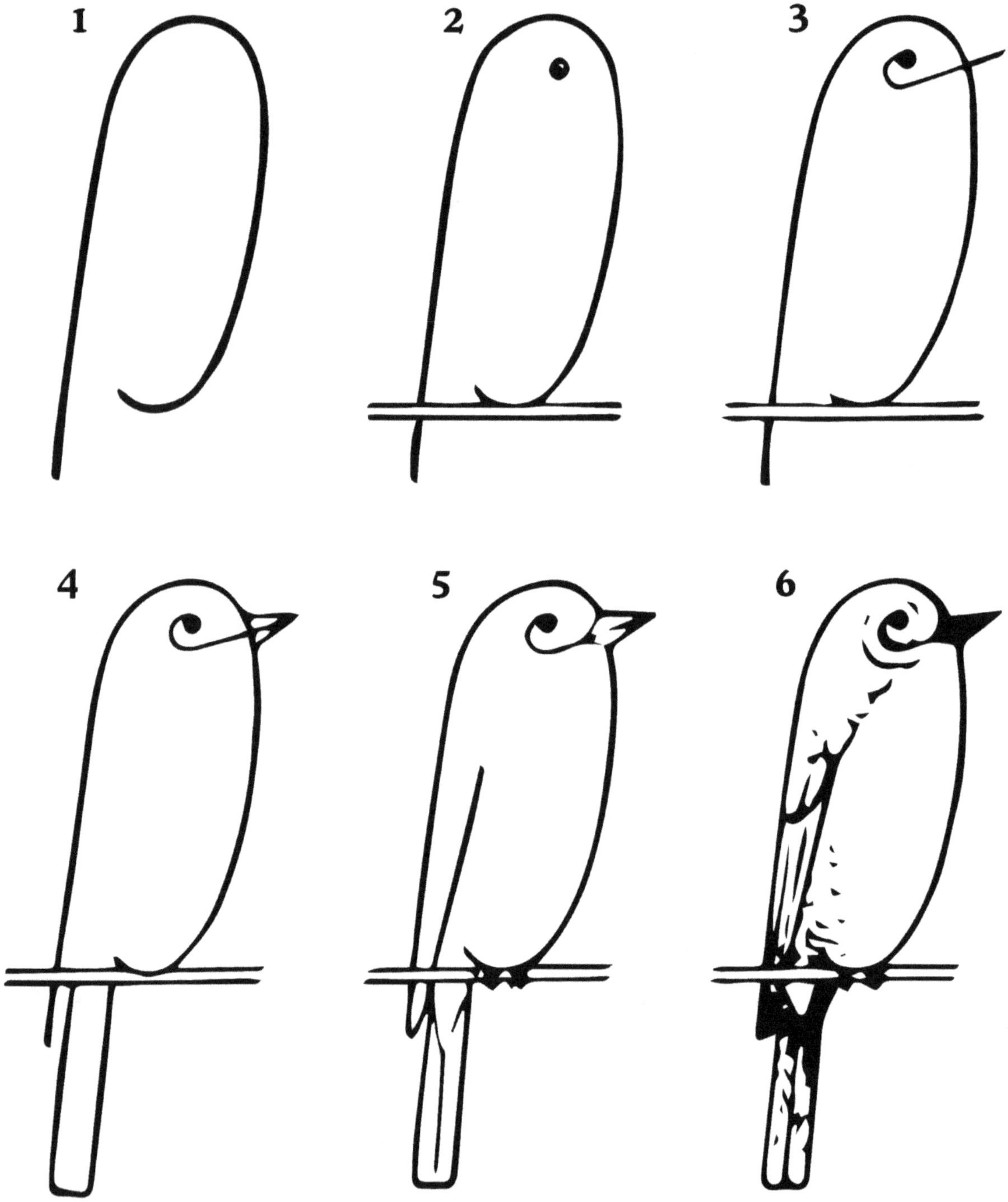
1
2
3
4
5
6

1

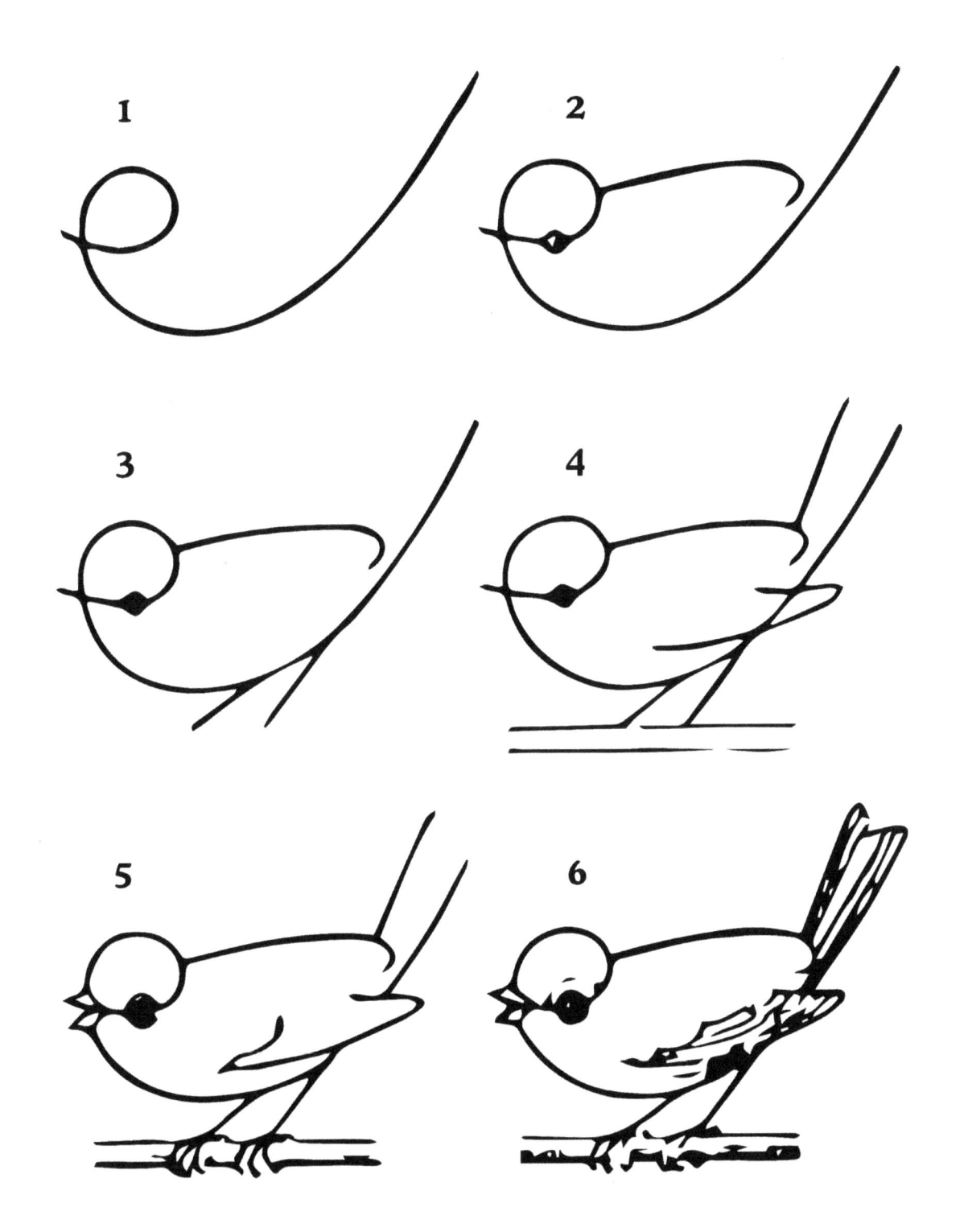

2

3

4

5

6

125

SECTION THREE
Creatures of The Water

LARGEMOUTH BASS

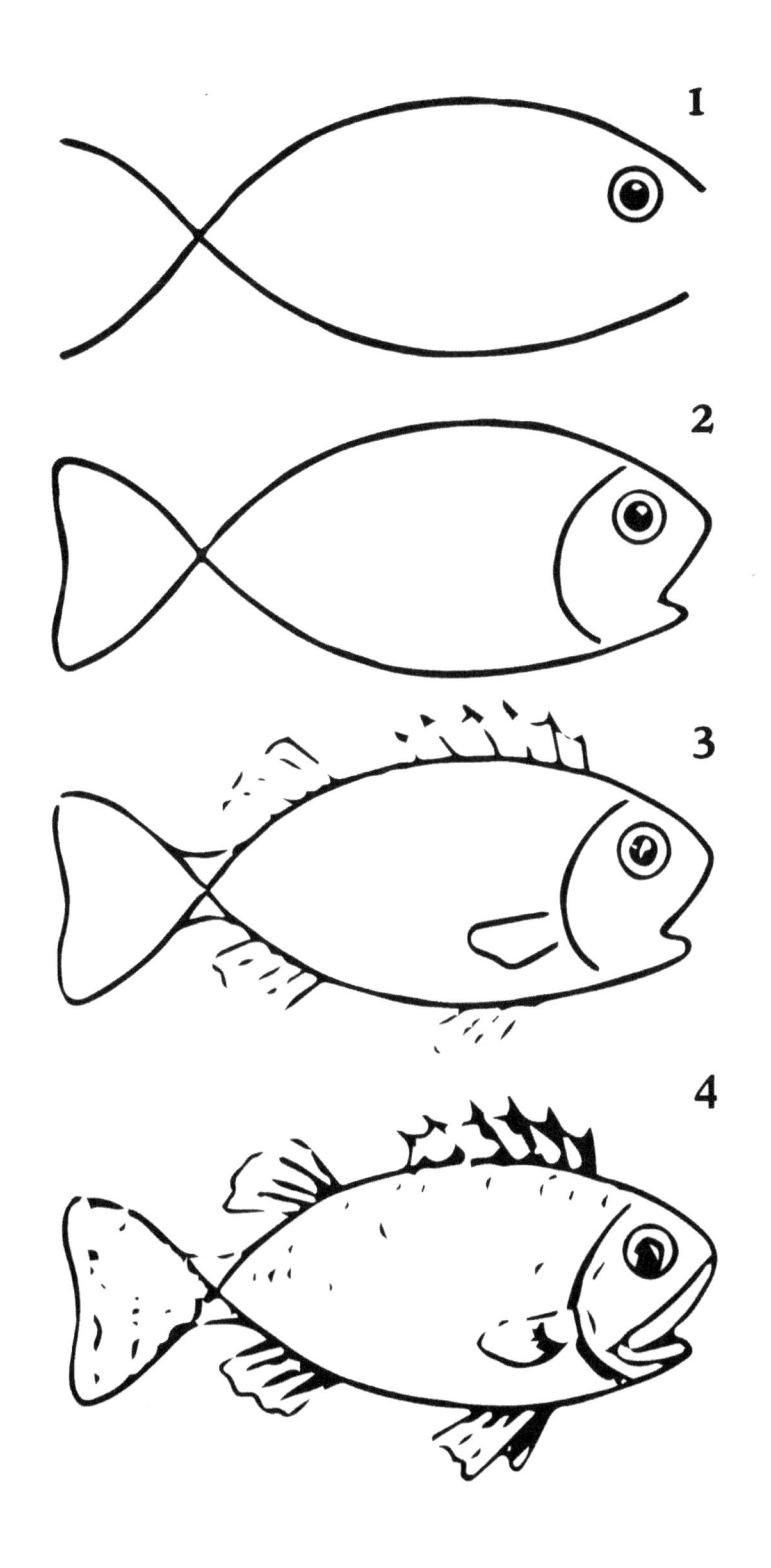

1
2
3
4

RED SEABREAM

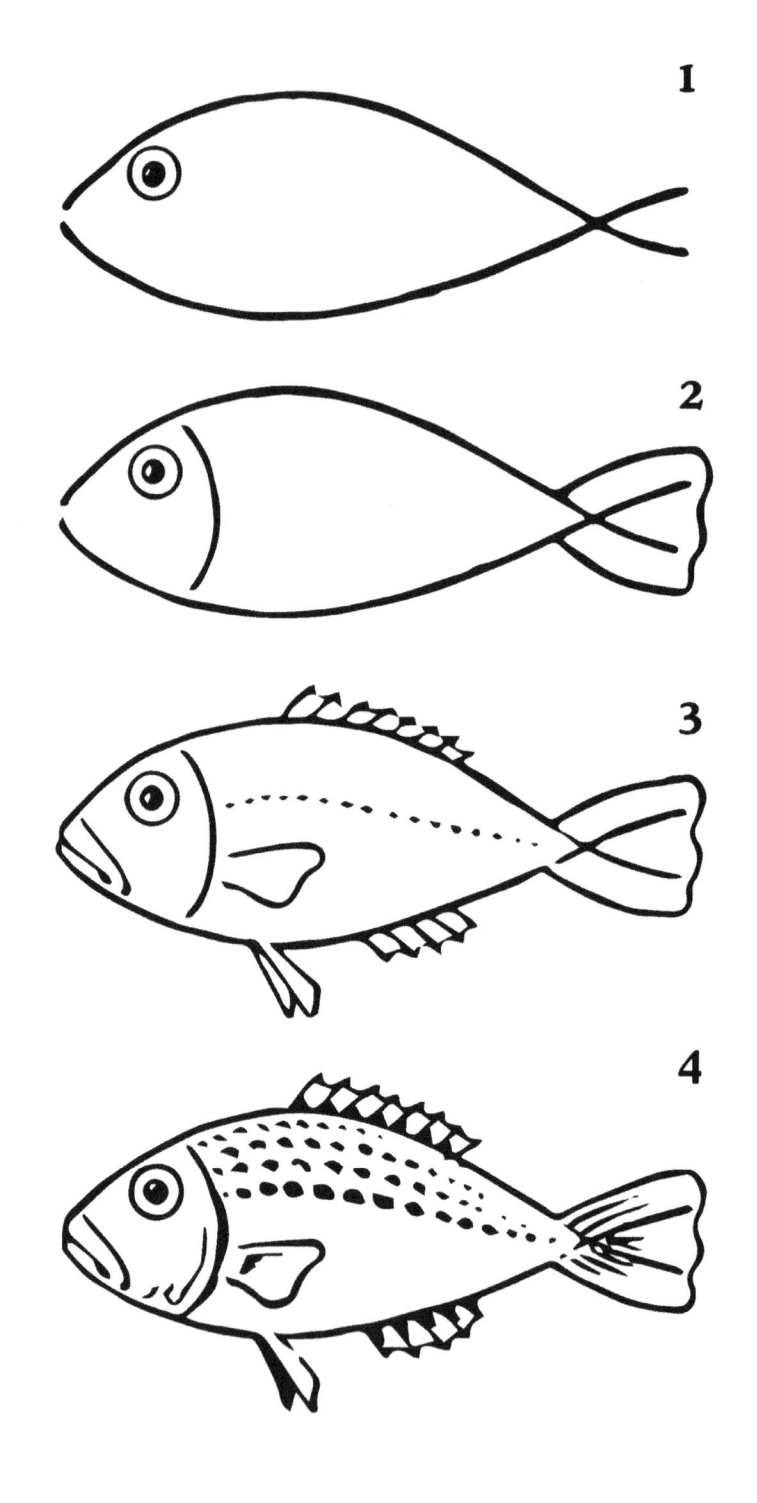

1

2

3

4

RED GURNARD

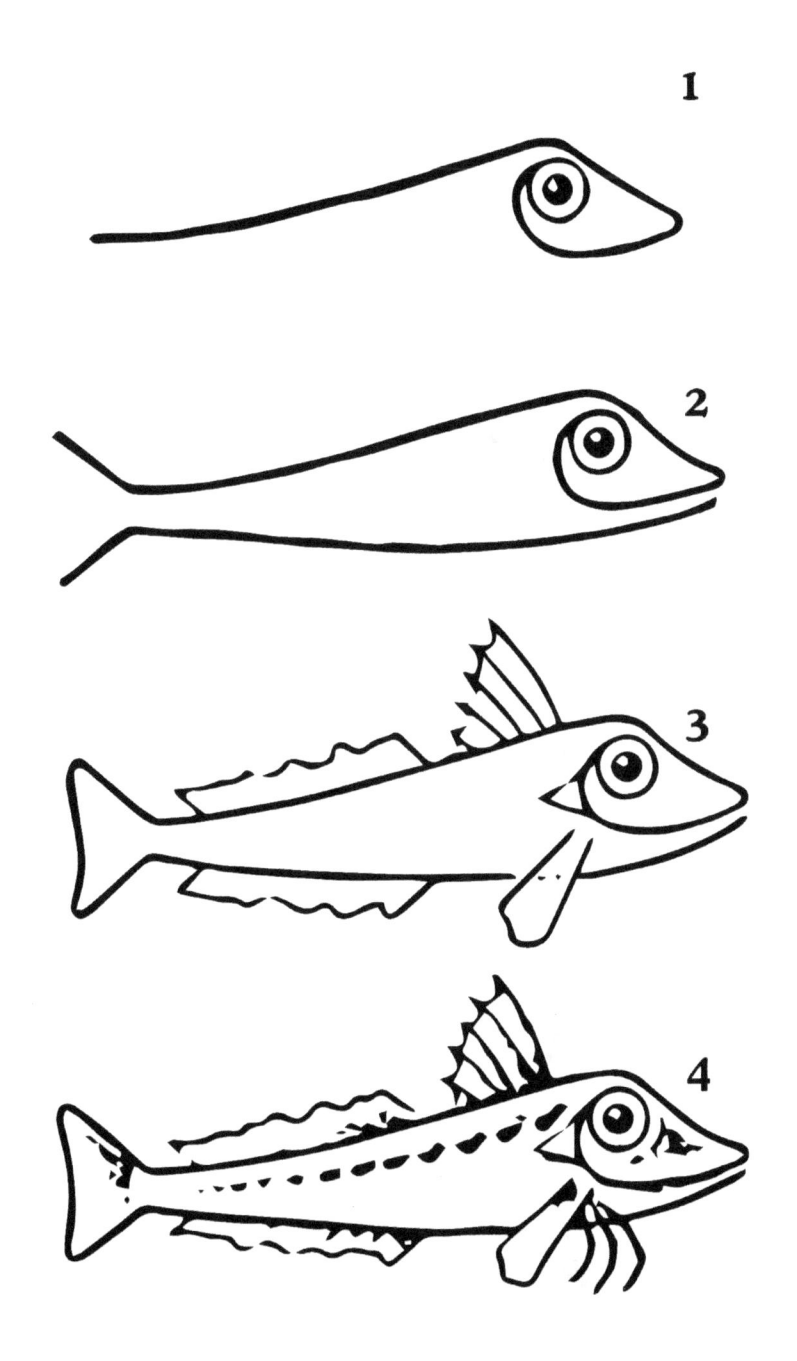

MILKFISH

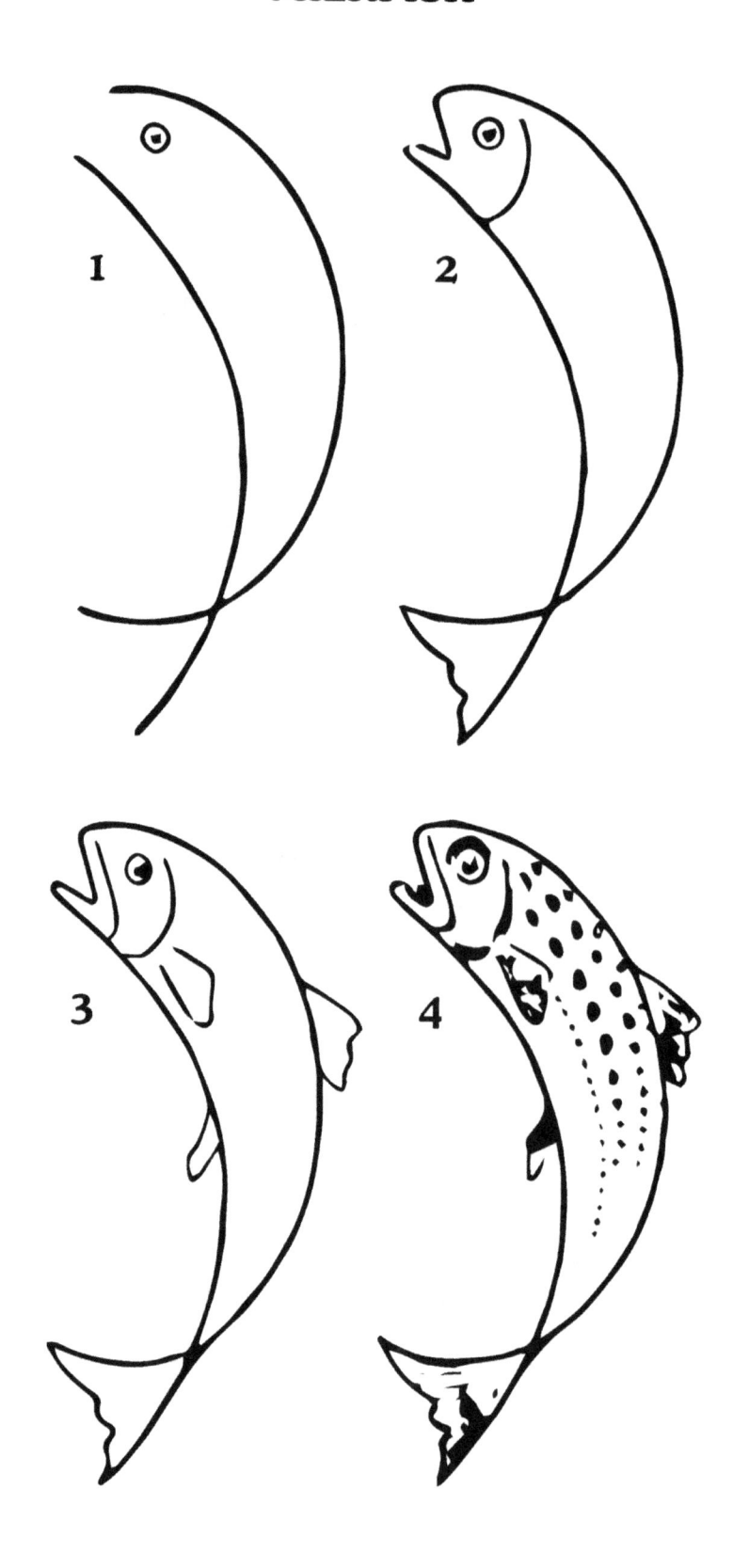

SHOREFISH

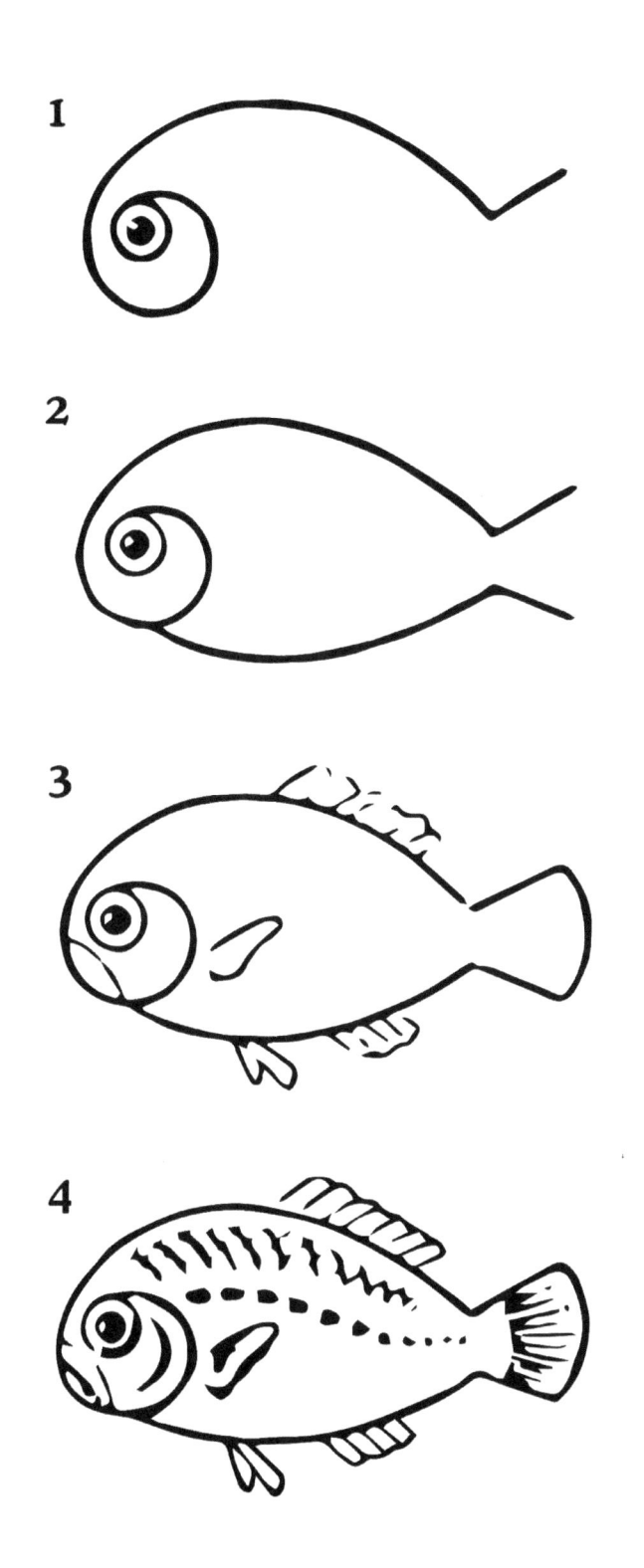

1

2

3

4

BLUEFISH

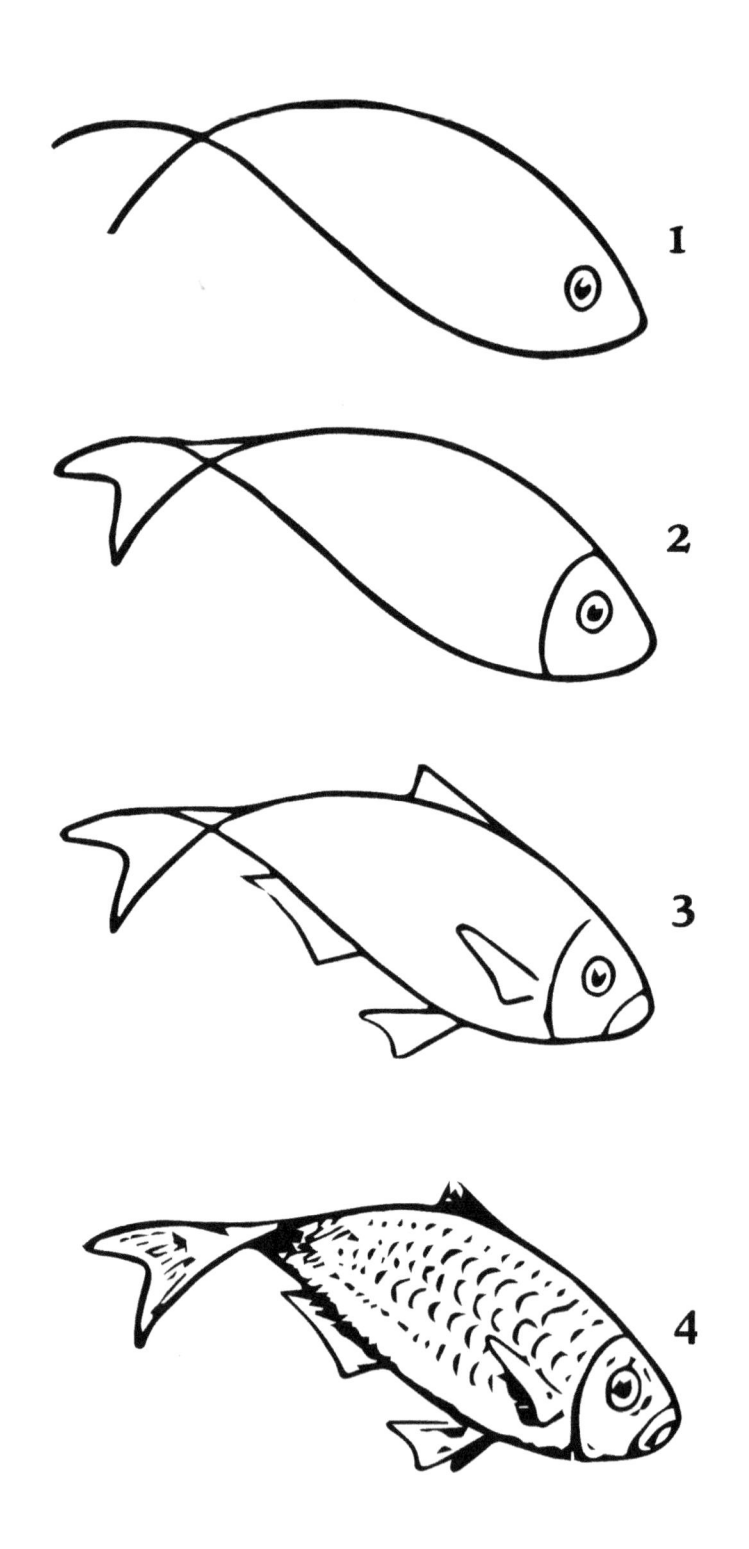

1
2
3
4

SHOREFISH

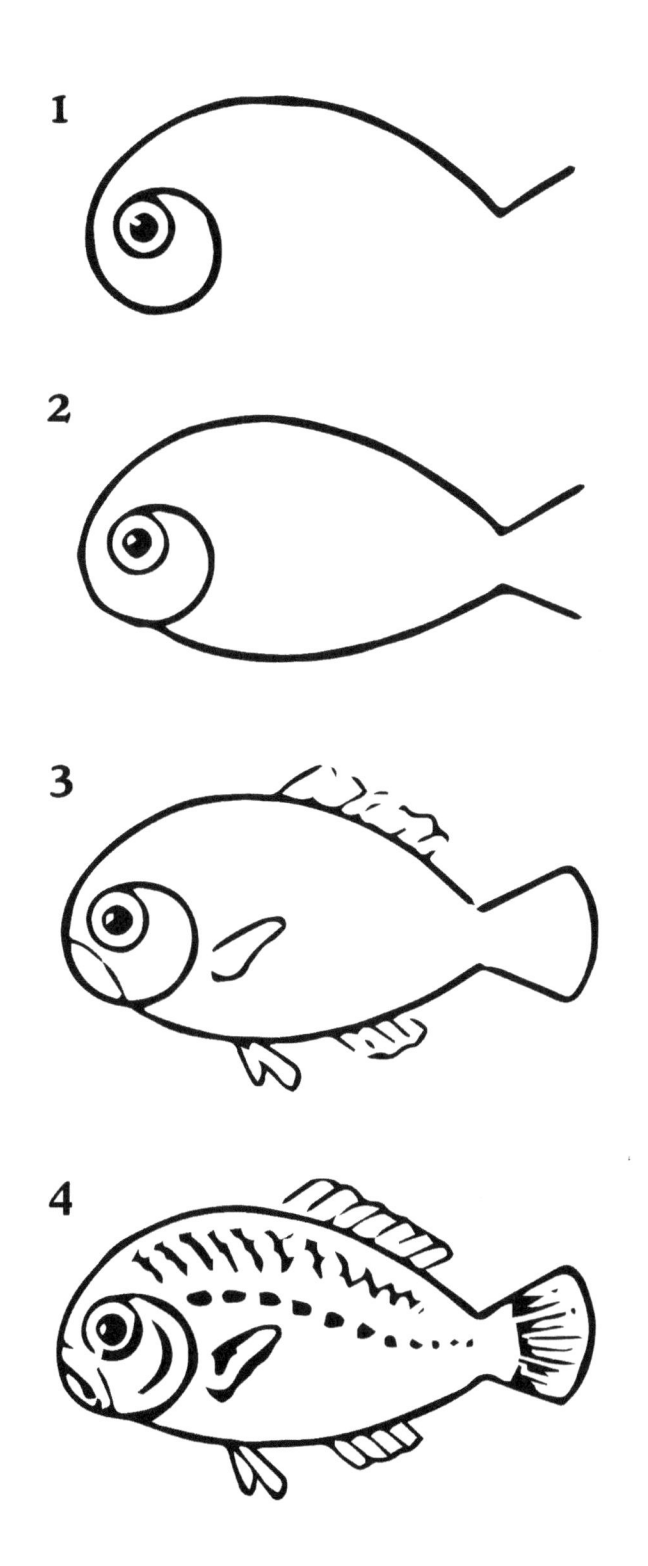

1
2
3
4

BLUEFISH

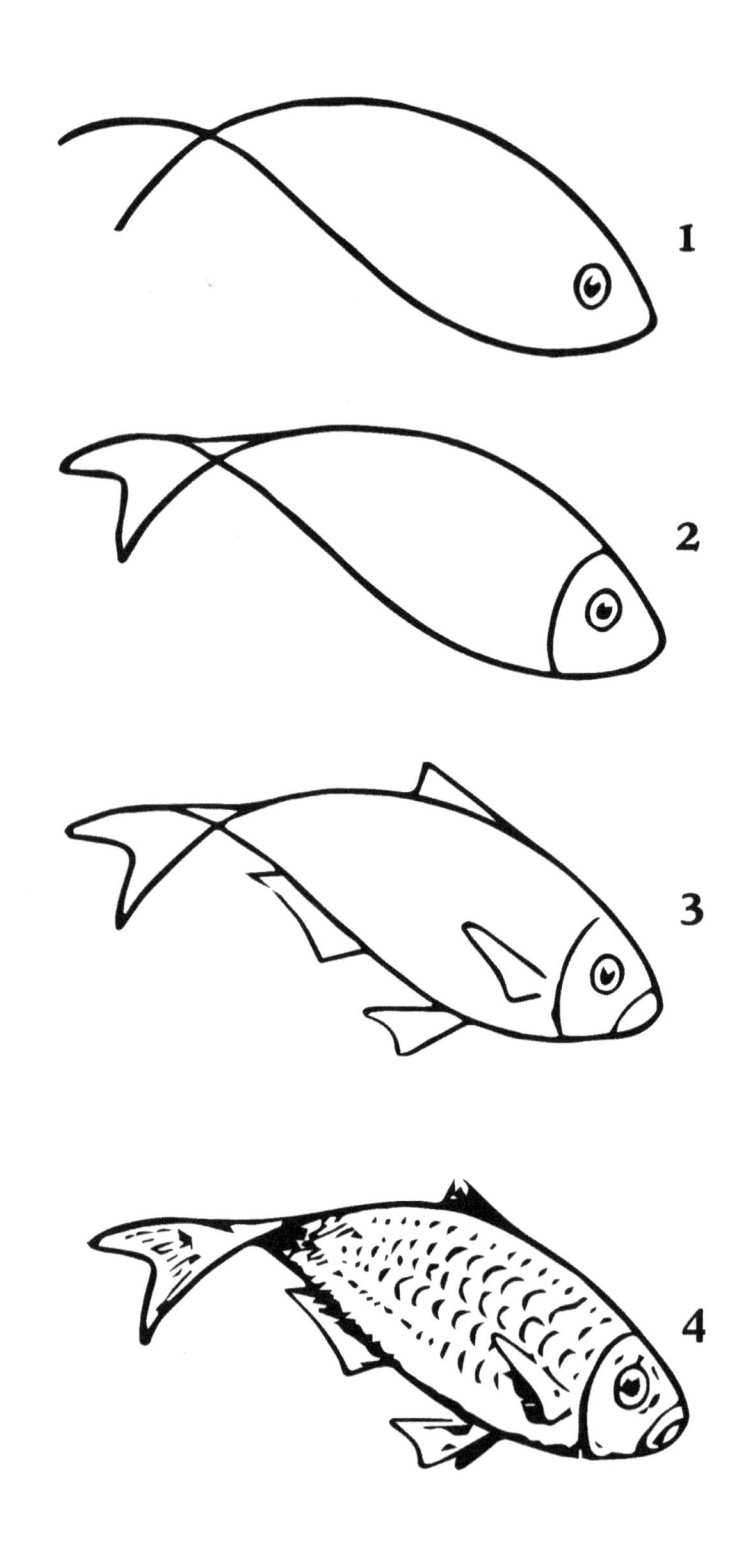

1
2
3
4

CURIOUS FISHES

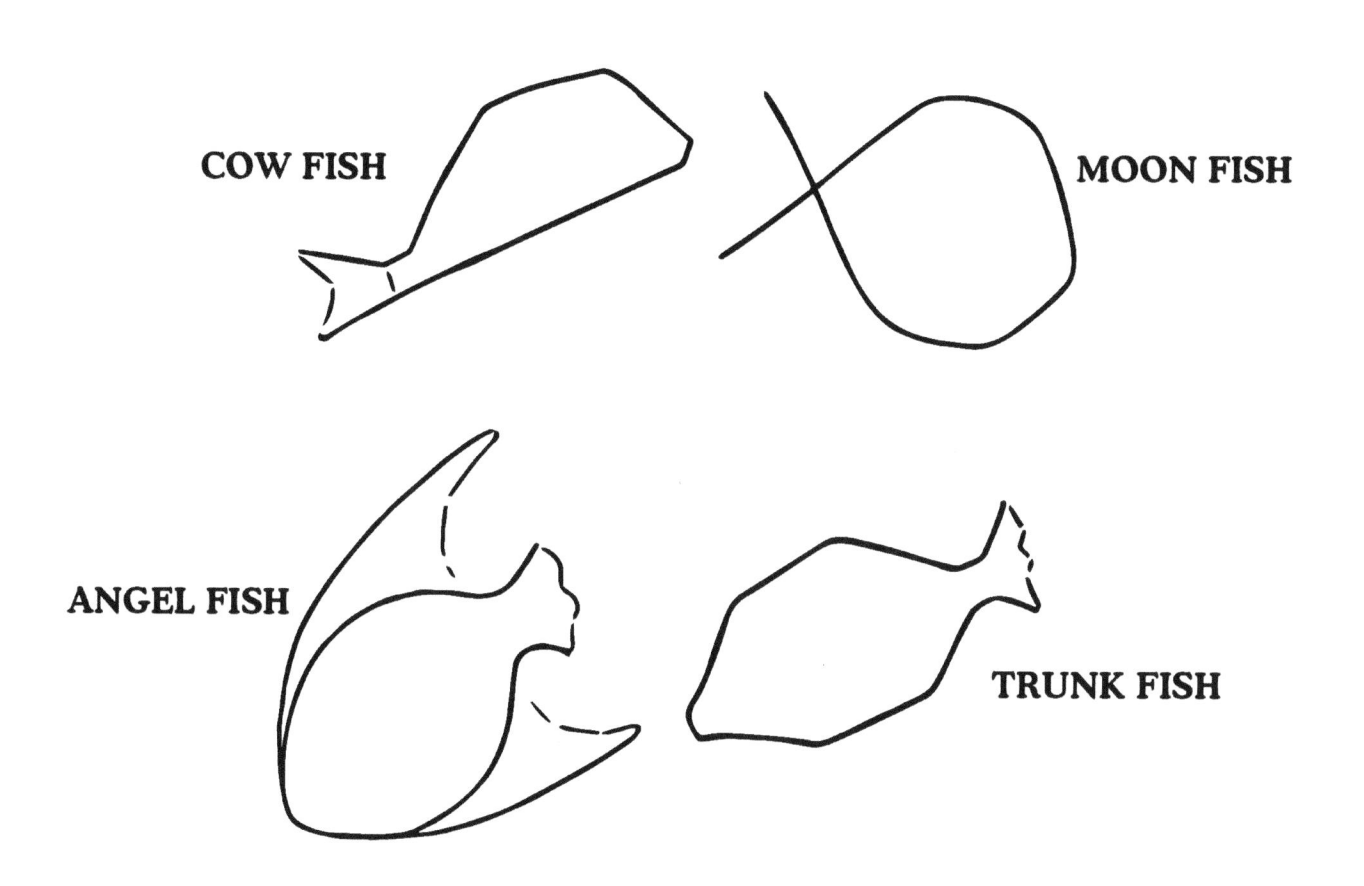

COW FISH

MOON FISH

ANGEL FISH

TRUNK FISH

1

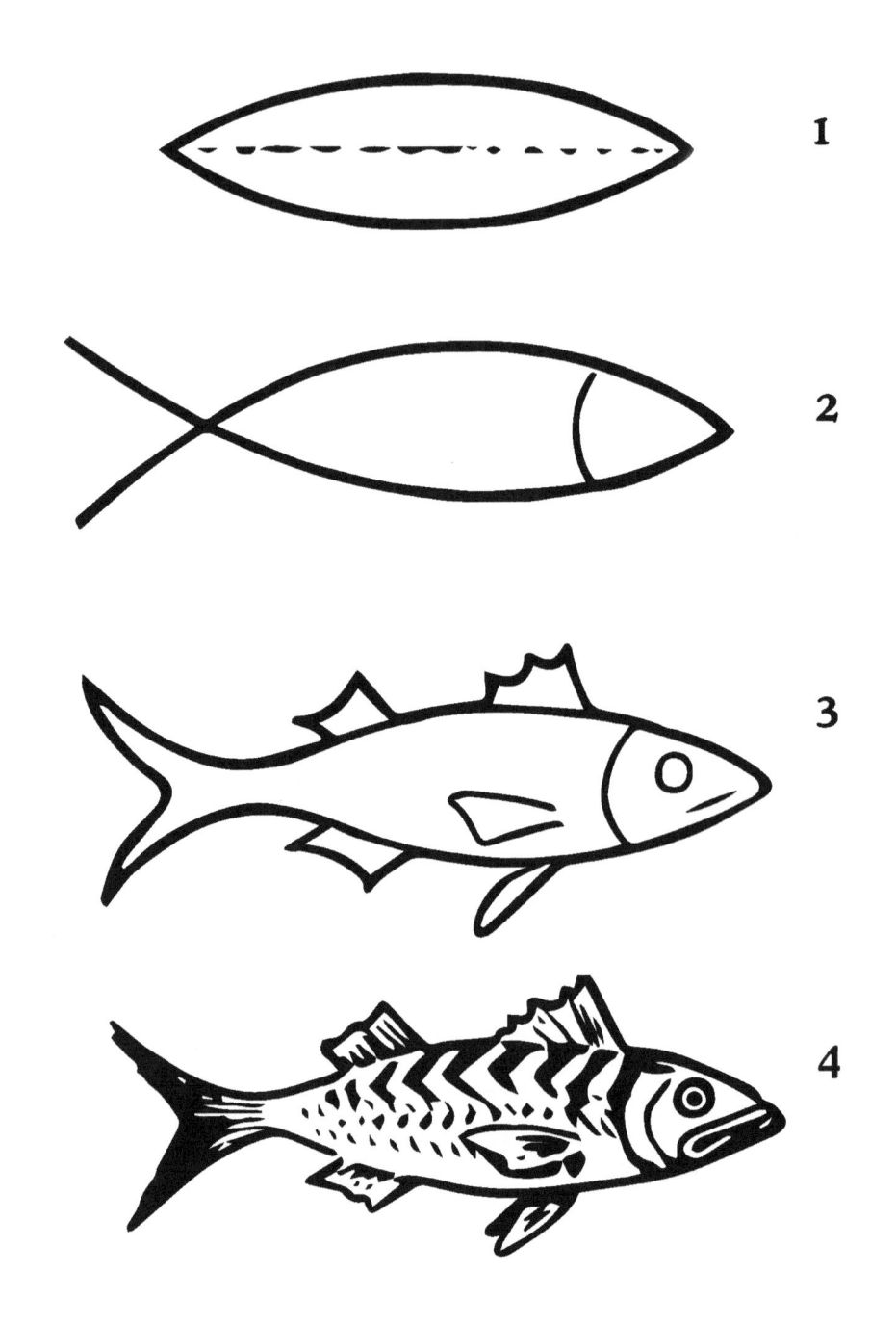

2

3

4

FLYING FISH

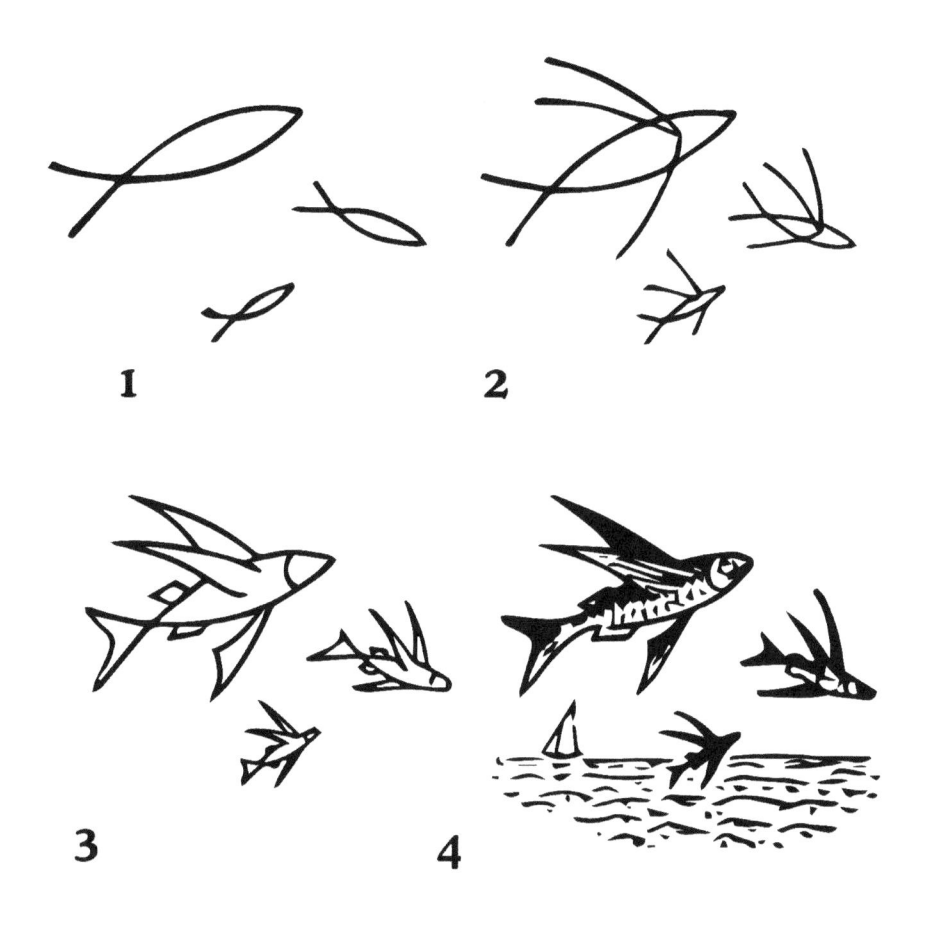

1

2

3

4

FROGS

1

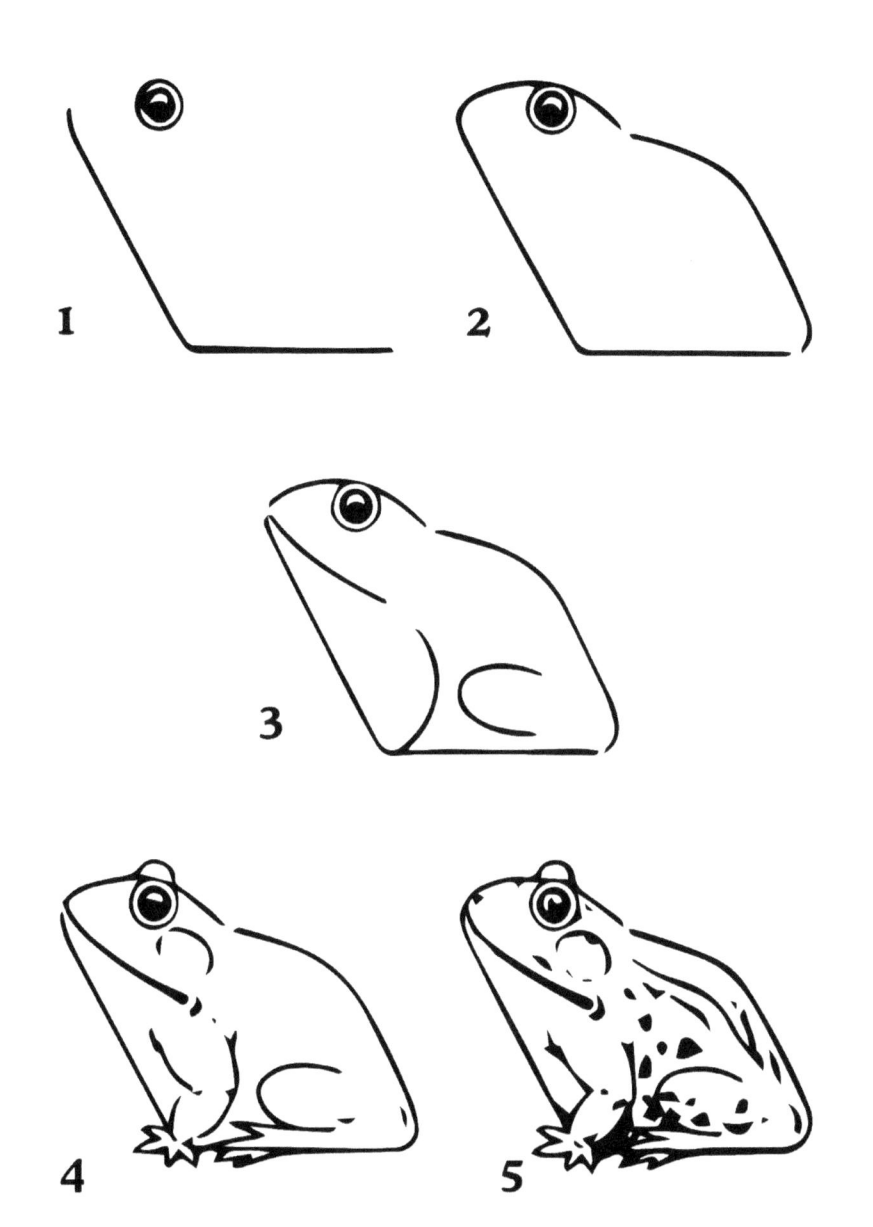

2

3

4

5

TADPOLES

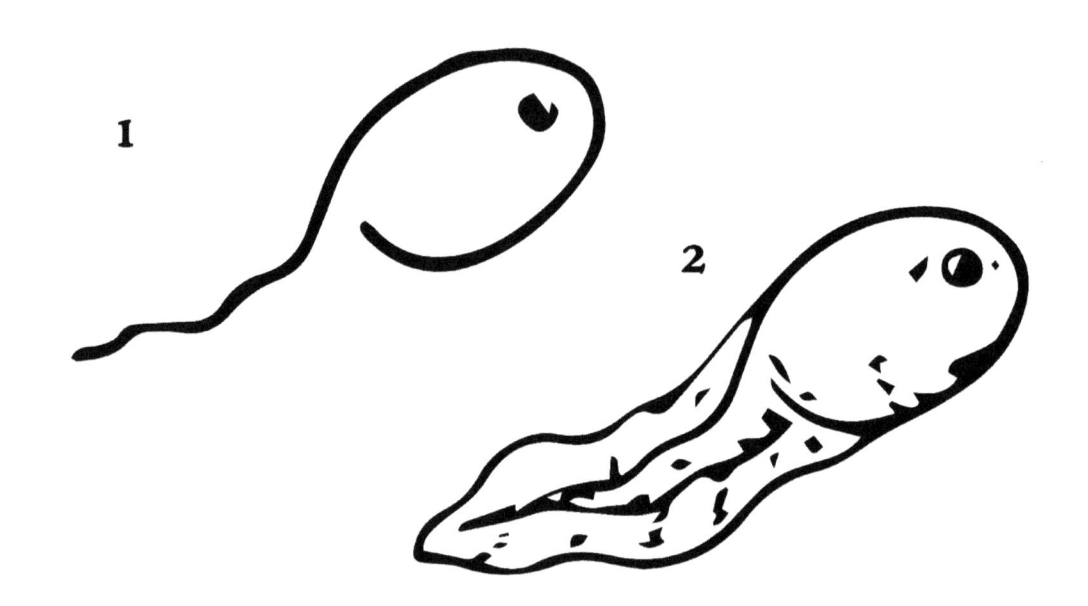

1

2

1

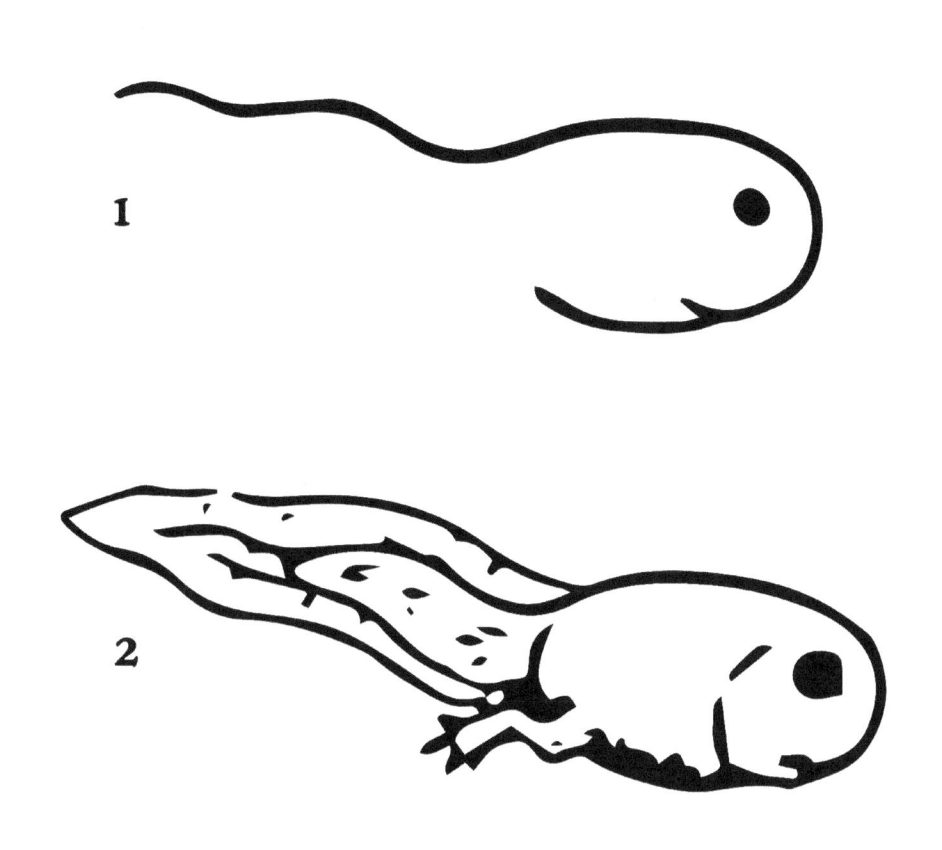

2

1

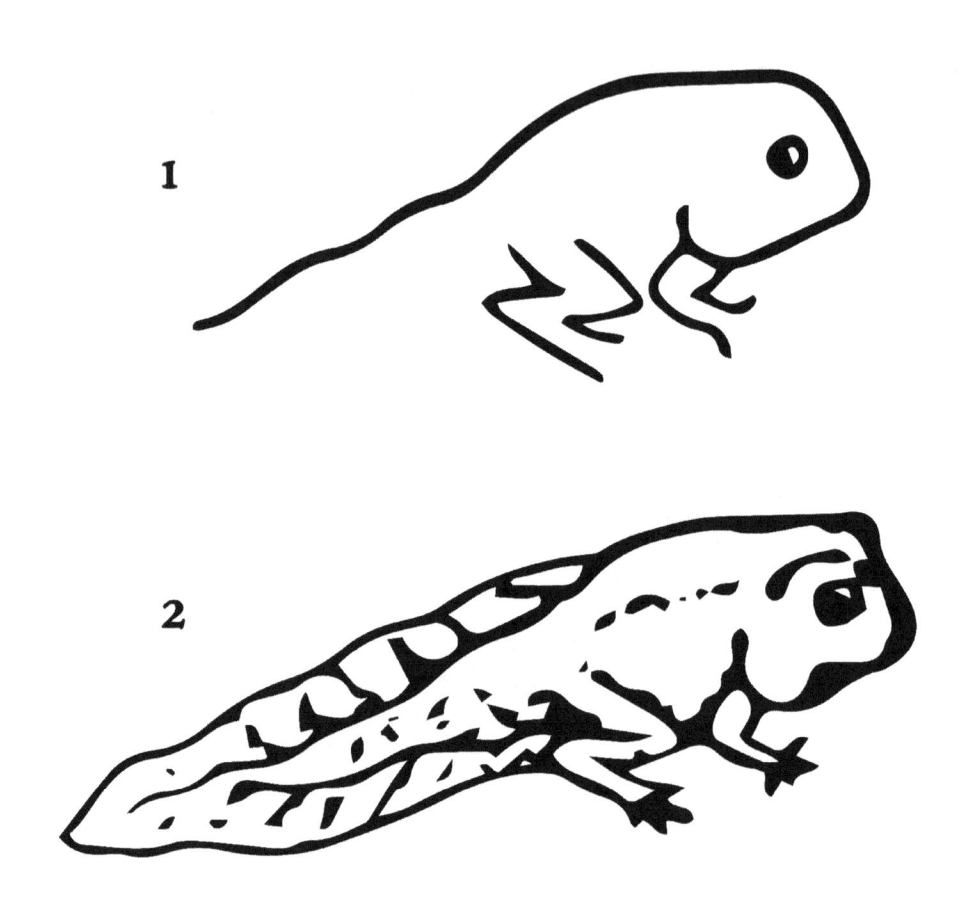

2

1

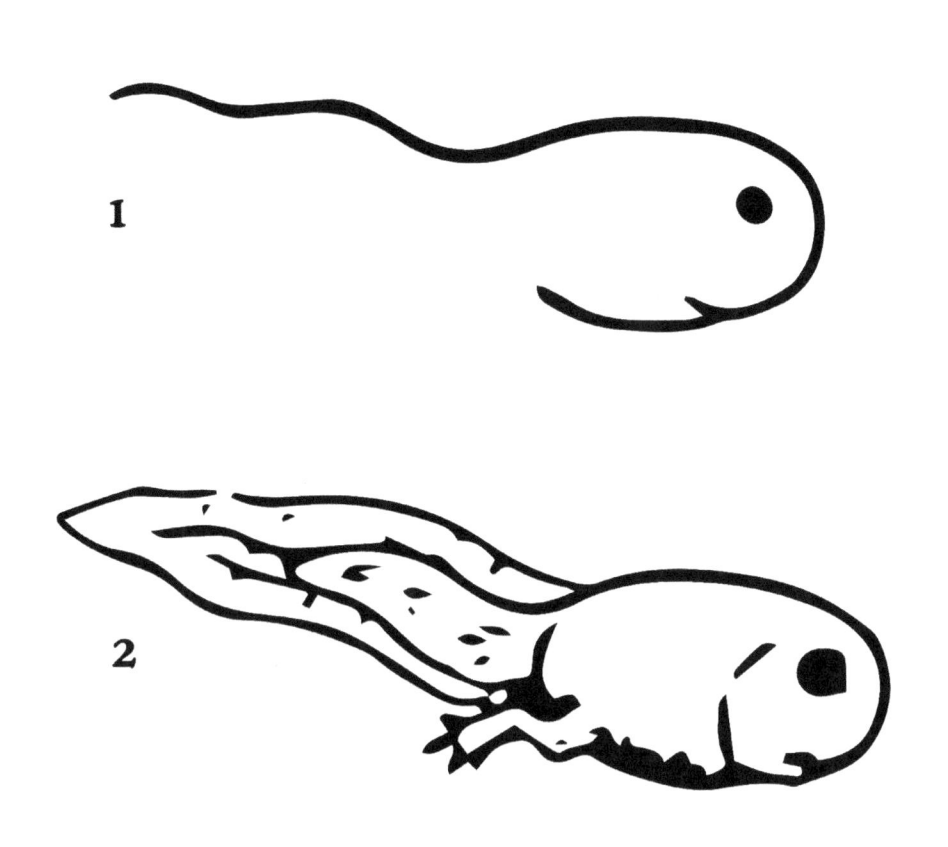

2

139

1

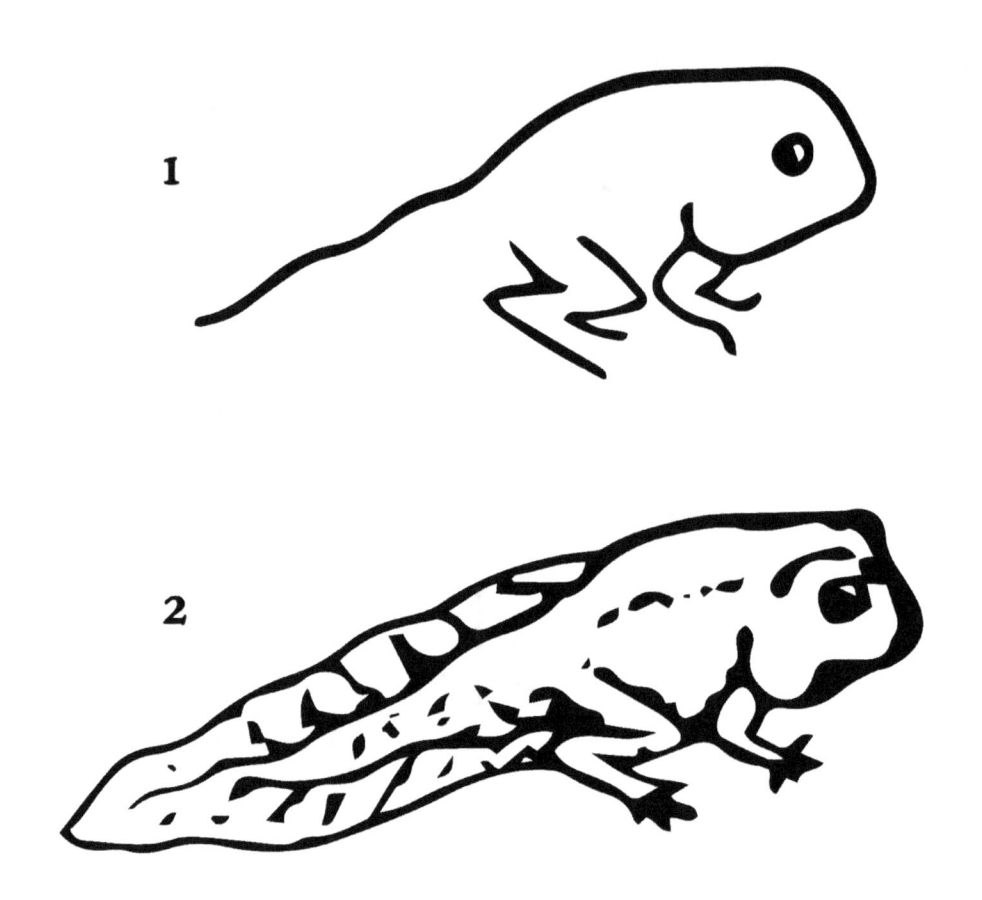

2

CRAB

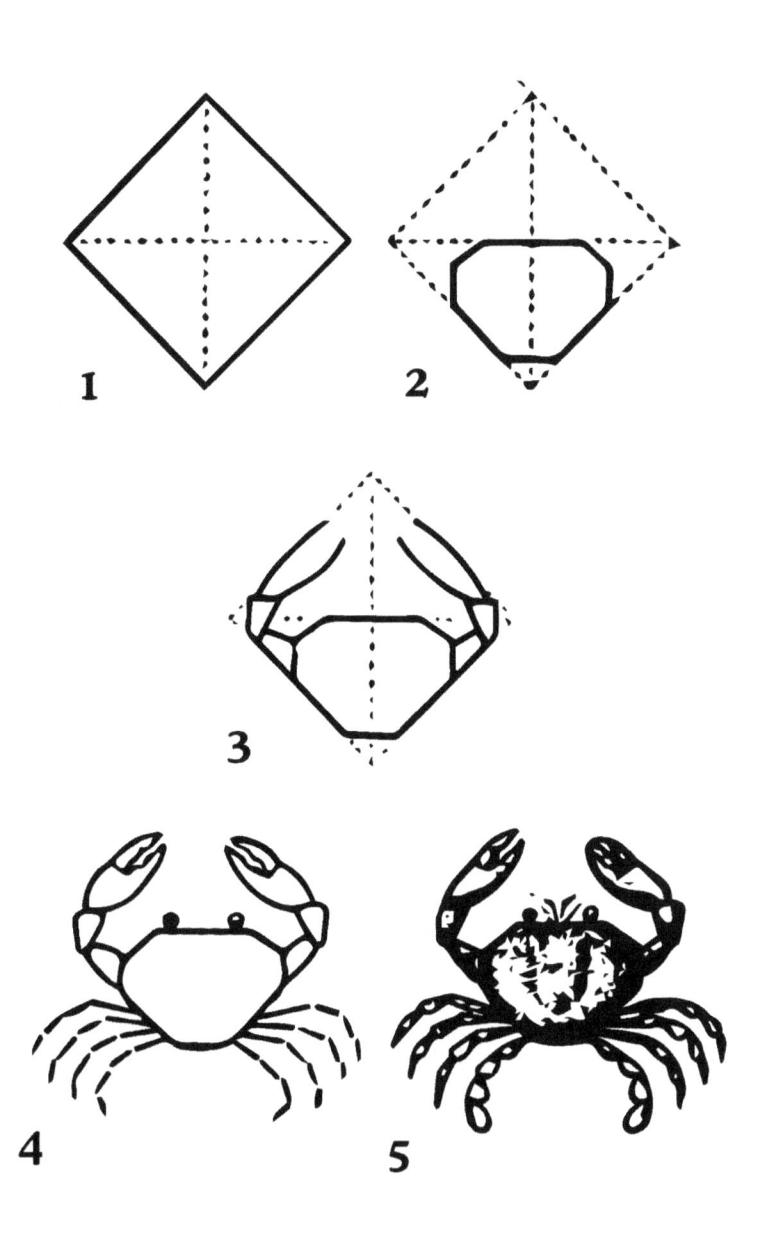

1
2
3
4
5

SEA HORSE

1
2
3

4
5

STAR FISH

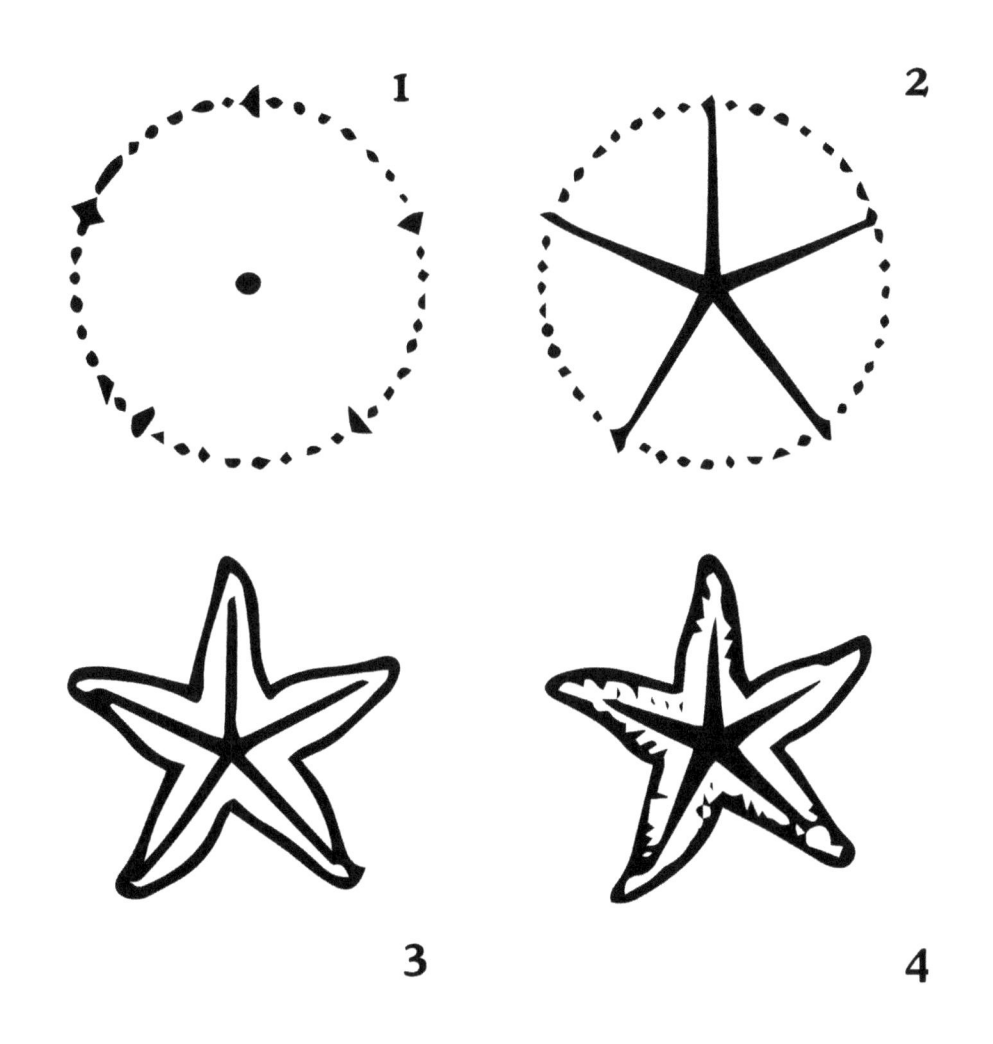

1

2

3

4

SUGGESTIONS FOR WATERCOLOR PAINTING

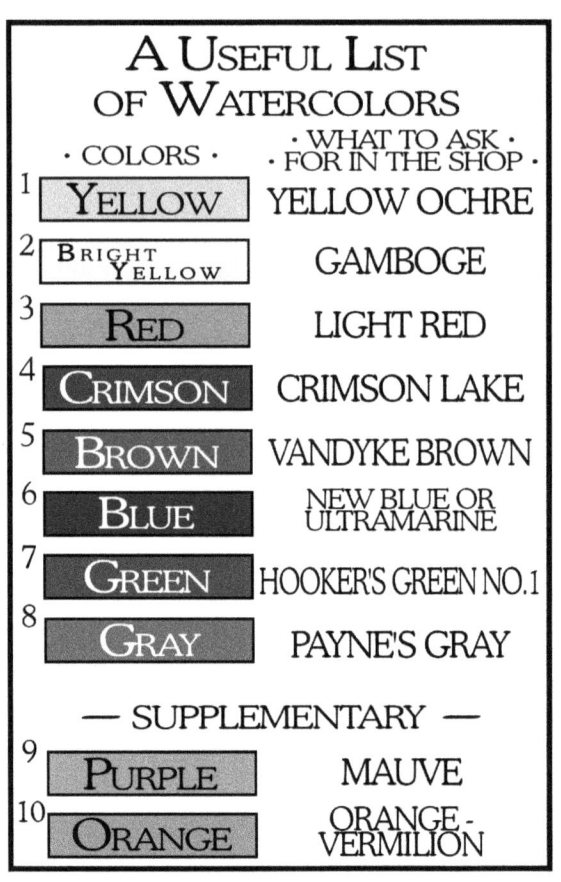

A Useful List of Watercolors

#	Colors	What to ask for in the shop
1	Yellow	YELLOW OCHRE
2	Bright Yellow	GAMBOGE
3	Red	LIGHT RED
4	Crimson	CRIMSON LAKE
5	Brown	VANDYKE BROWN
6	Blue	NEW BLUE OR ULTRAMARINE
7	Green	HOOKER'S GREEN NO. 1
8	Gray	PAYNE'S GRAY
— SUPPLEMENTARY —		
9	Purple	MAUVE
10	Orange	ORANGE-VERMILION

Here is a good list of colors for practical work. The first eight are enough for every purpose; but add if you wish, purple and orange. Moist colors in pans are best. There are many different kinds of red, green, blue and brown paints; and as you may be puzzled and not know what to get, the names of the best hues of these particular colors are also given. The most useful paints in this list are yellow ochre, light red, Vandyke brown and Payne's gray. Learn to work with them, use them often and see the beautiful effects they produce. Delicate tints are made with thin washes of yellow ochre and light red. Vandyke brown makes a variety of pleasing tints.

Use the bright colors sparingly.

You do not need black paint. Payne's gray with either brown, blue, crimson or green gives rich dark tones. Payne's gray is also useful in shadows and shading other colors. For the different kinds of greens, mix yellow ochre, blue or brown with Hooker's green. Use thin washes of light red and blue for the gray of distances and clouds.

OTHER BOOKS
FROM IRONPOWER PUBLISHING

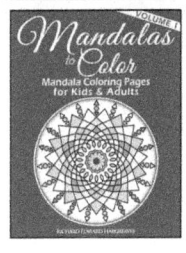

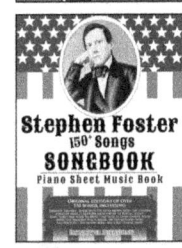

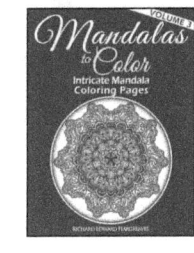

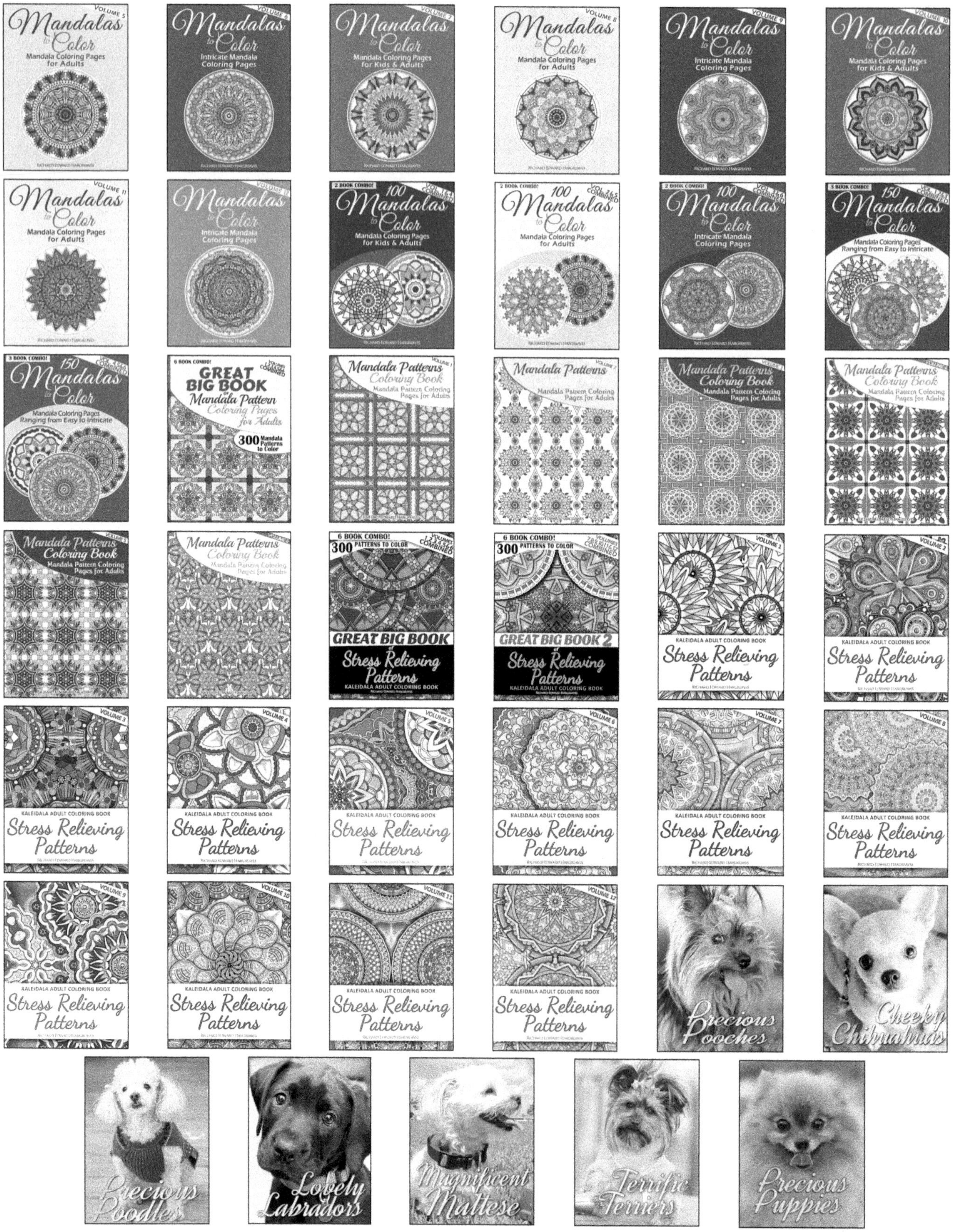
Mandalas to Color
Mandala Coloring Pages for Adults
Intricate Mandala Coloring Pages
Mandala Coloring Pages for Kids & Adults
2 BOOK COMBO!
100 Mandalas to Color
3 BOOK COMBO!
150 Mandalas to Color
Mandala Coloring Pages Ranging from Easy to Intricate
9 BOOK COMBO!
GREAT BIG BOOK
Mandala Pattern Coloring Pages for Adults
300 Mandala Patterns to Color
Mandala Patterns Coloring Book
Mandala Pattern Coloring Pages for Adults
6 BOOK COMBO!
300 PATTERNS TO COLOR
GREAT BIG BOOK of Stress Relieving Patterns
GREAT BIG BOOK 2 of Stress Relieving Patterns
KALEIDALA ADULT COLORING BOOK
Stress Relieving Patterns
Precious Pooches
Cheeky Chihuahuas
Precious Poodles
Lovely Labradors
Magnificent Maltese
Terrific Terriers
Precious Puppies

CPSIA information can be obtained
at www.ICGtesting.com
Printed in the USA
LVHW021301201218
601203LV00011B/715